THE APOLLO MISSIONS FOR KIDS

with 21 Activities

The People and Engineering
Behind the Race to the Moon

Jerome Pohlen

CHICAGO
REVIEW
PRESS

For Joe, Mike, and Paul
Pohlen, and Leonard Popp,
who all worked on Apollo.

Copyright © 2019 by Jerome Pohlen
All rights reserved
Published by Chicago Review Press Incorporated
814 North Franklin Street
Chicago, Illinois 60610
ISBN 978-0-912777-17-7

Library of Congress Cataloging-in-Publication Data
Names: Pohlen, Jerome, author.
Title: The Apollo missions for kids : the people and engineering
    behind the race to the moon with 21 activities / Jerome
    Pohlen.
Description: Chicago, Illinois : Chicago Review Press
    Incorporated, [2019] | Includes bibliographical references and
    index.
Identifiers: LCCN 2019009475 (print) | LCCN 2019012008 (ebook)
    | ISBN 9780912777184 (PDF edition) | ISBN 9780912777191
    (EPUB edition) | ISBN 9780912777207 (Kindle edition) |
    ISBN 9780912777177 (trade pbk. edition) | ISBN 9780912777177
    (trade pbk. edition : alk. paper)
Subjects: LCSH: Project Apollo (U.S.)—Juvenile literature. | Space
    flight to the moon—United States—History—20th century—
    Juvenile literature. | Aeronautics—Experiments—Juvenile
    literature.
Classification: LCC TL789.8.U6 (ebook) | LCC TL789.8.U6 A5688
    2019 (print) | DDC 629.45/4—dc23
LC record available at https://lccn.loc.gov/2019009475

Cover and interior design: Sarah Olson
Cover images: (front cover, clockwise from upper right) Apollo 9
docking illustration, courtesy of NASA, S69-18546; Apollo 17 rover
and lander, courtesy of NASA, AS17-147-22527; Apollo 9 simula-
tion training, courtesy of NASA, S69-19981; Apollo 15 launch,
courtesy of NASA, S71-41810; Apollo 11 pin, author's collection;
Apollo 8 reentry illustration, courtesy of NASA, S68-55292; Apollo
15 astronaut and flag, courtesy of NASA, AS15-88-11866; the moon
as seen from Apollo 16, Wikimedia Commons/NASA; (back cover,
clockwise from upper left) Apollo 11 lander in orbit, courtesy of
NASA, AS11-44-6581; Apollo 8 separation illustration, courtesy of
NASA, S68-51306; full moon, 123RF.com, © Cristian Cestaro

Interior illustrations: Lindsey Cleworth Schauer

Printed in the United States of America
5 4 3 2 1

Courtesy of NASA, 69PC-0397

CONTENTS

TIME LINE

1926 **March 16,** Robert Goddard launches first liquid-fuel rocket

1957 **October 4,** Sputnik launches

1961 **April 12,** Yuri Gagarin flight
May 5, Mercury, *Freedom 7*
May 25, Kennedy issues moon challenge
July 21, Mercury, *Liberty Bell 7*

1962 **February 20,** Mercury, *Friendship 7*
May 24, Mercury, *Aurora 7*
October 3, Mercury, *Sigma 7*

1963 **May 15–16,** Mercury, *Faith 7*

1965 **March 23,** Gemini 3
June 3–7, Gemini 4
August 21–29, Gemini 5
December 4–18, Gemini 7
December 15–16, Gemini 6

1966 **March 16–17,** Gemini 8
June 3–6, Gemini 9
July 18–21, Gemini 10
September 12–15, Gemini 11
November 11–15, Gemini 12

1967 **January 27,** Apollo 1 fire
November 9, Apollo 4

1968 **January 22–23,** Apollo 5
April 4, Apollo 6
October 11–22, Apollo 7
December 21–27, Apollo 8

1969 **March 3–13,** Apollo 9
May 18–26, Apollo 10
July 16–24, Apollo 11
November 14–24, Apollo 12

Apollo 15 on the moon. *Courtesy of NASA/Lunar and Planetary Institute, AS15-87-11805 through AS15-87-11824*

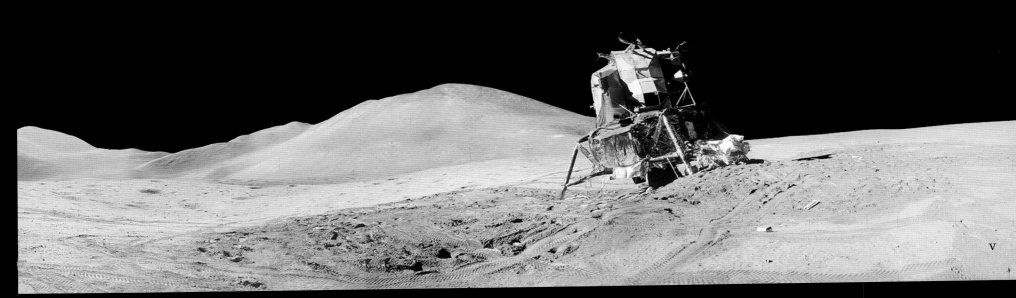

v

INTRODUCTION

ONE LONG STEP

Four hours after Apollo 12 landed on the moon, astronauts Pete Conrad and Alan Bean were ready to go outside. Conrad went first, crawling backward through the hatch as Bean guided him.

"Doing good. You're headed right square out the hatch. You'll have to bend over more, though," said Bean. "Wait. Wait. Wait. Oops. Come forward a little. Move to your right, you're . . . there you are. Now go. . . . You got to kneel down a little more. . . . Well, I'll push you if you don't mind."

Finally, kneeling on the platform outside the hatch, Conrad waited for Mission Control to tell him the television camera was working. "We've got TV," came the word from Houston. "No Pete Conrad as yet." The astronaut had yet to move into camera view.

Bean continued to guide Conrad until he reached the top of the ladder. "Adios," Bean said, as Conrad crawled away. Rung by rung, Conrad descended as millions around the world watched. Four months earlier, when Apollo 11's Neil Armstrong first stepped on the moon, he proclaimed, "That's one small step for man, one giant leap for mankind." Now it was Conrad's turn. What profound message would he deliver at this, the second Apollo landing?

"Whoopie!" shouted Conrad after dropping the last step. "Man, that may have been a small one for Neil, but that's a long one for me!"

Conrad carefully stepped away from the ladder, checked his footing, and looked at the bright, lifeless moonscape. And there, in the distance, he spotted another spacecraft.

"Sometimes it seems that Apollo came before its time," said astronaut Gene Cernan, years after he walked on the moon. "President Kennedy reached far into the 21st century, grabbed a decade of time, and slipped it neatly into the 1960s and 1970s."

It was an enormous team effort. More than 400,000 people worked on Apollo in factories and offices spread out over 46 states. It cost US taxpayers $24 billion, about $150 billion in today's dollars. By the time the last capsule splashed down, NASA had made eleven manned Apollo flights, six of which landed on the moon, and brought back 842 pounds of lunar rocks and soil.

Twenty-nine astronauts flew Apollo missions, twenty-four went to the moon, and twelve walked on its surface. Eight died before they ever got the chance.

Apollo was a bold, complicated, dangerous, and expensive adventure. But as Pete Conrad knew, it was also a lot of fun.

Courtesy of NASA, AS12-48-7136

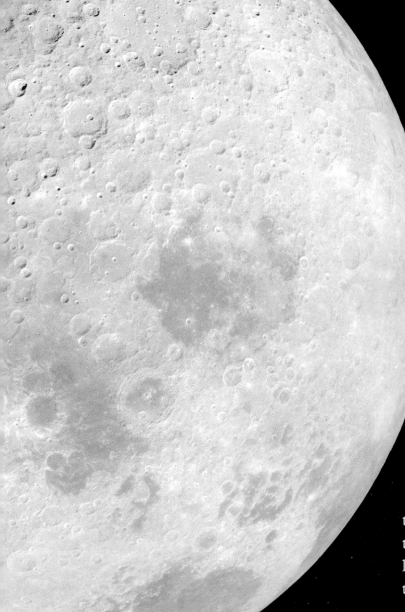

1

The Challenge

May 25, 1961. It was called a "Special Message to Congress on Urgent National Needs." President John F. Kennedy had just taken office and was outlining his priorities for the coming years. He spoke about job retraining, military spending, nuclear disarmament, and other issues. But what he said at the end of his speech surprised lawmakers and everyone else who was listening.

"Now is the time to take longer strides—time for a great new American enterprise—time for this nation to take a clearly leading role in space achievements, which in many ways may hold the key to our future on Earth," he said. "I believe that this nation should commit itself to achieving the goal, before this decade is out, of landing a man on the moon and returning him safely to the Earth. No single space project in this period will be more impressive to mankind, or more important for the long-range exploration of space. And none will be so difficult or expensive to accomplish."

President Kennedy addresses Congress, May 25, 1961. *Courtesy of NASA, 70-H-1075*

What did he say?

Just 20 days earlier, the United States had successfully launched its first astronaut—Alan Shepard—into space. The flight lasted just 15 minutes and 28 seconds and didn't even go into orbit.

"I thought [Kennedy] was crazy," said NASA's Chris Kraft. "I thought he'd lost his mind." Kraft had been the flight director (the leader at Mission

Control) during Shepard's flight. He understood the immense challenge that Kennedy had laid before them. And all in less than nine years.

To the Moon

The idea of going to the moon was nothing new. In the second century AD, an Assyrian writer named Lucian of Samosata wrote a novel, *A True History*, about a ship that was swept up in a tornado and dropped on the moon. Once there, the sailors found men riding three-headed vultures who were battling inhabitants from the sun. *A True History* is the first known work of science fiction.

Others would write about lunar voyages, but it wasn't until 1865, when Jules Verne published *From the Earth to the Moon*, that science fiction came anywhere near science fact. In the story, three men from the Baltimore Gun Club journey to the moon in a capsule fired from a 900-foot-long cannon. The French novel ended with the crew orbiting the moon, and readers demanded a sequel. *Around the Moon* (1870) saw the men and their capsule splashing down in the Pacific Ocean, where they were rescued by the US Navy.

Verne's understanding of science made his novels unique. He correctly calculated the speed a spacecraft would need to escape the Earth's gravity, described the weightlessness of space travel, and more.

The books were bestsellers and inspired many of the first space scientists and engineers. "My interest in space travel was first aroused by the famous writer of fantasies, Jules Verne," wrote Konstantin

Tsiolkovsky. "He directed my thoughts along certain channels, then came a desire, and after that, the work of the mind."

Tsiolkovsky, a deaf Russian schoolteacher and physics researcher, published *Exploration of the Cosmos in Rocket-Powered Vehicles* in May 1903, seven months before the Wright brothers' first powered airplane flight. It was the first book to describe spaceflight mathematically. Tsiolkovsky also wrote about liquid fuels, "rocket trains" (multi-stage rockets), weightlessness, air locks, and even the possibility of life on other planets.

Verne also inspired American Robert Goddard. In 1899, when he was 17 years old, Goddard was told to trim the branches of a cherry tree behind his family's barn in Worcester, Massachusetts. Up in its branches, he daydreamed. "I imagined how wonderful it would be to make some device which had even the *possibility* of ascending to Mars, and how it would look on a small scale, if sent up from the meadow at my feet," he later wrote.

On March 16, 1926, after years of failed attempts, he launched the world's first liquid-fuel rocket from his Aunt Effie Ward's farm in Auburn, Massachusetts. It flew 41 feet high and landed 184 feet away, in a cabbage patch. In time he would design rockets that soared as high as 9,000 feet— almost two miles. Today Goddard is known as the "Father of Modern Rocketry."

Others followed: Robert Esnault-Pelterie of France, Hermann Oberth of Germany, and Wernher von Braun, also of Germany. Von Braun developed the first reliable liquid-fuel rocket, the V-2, during World War II. Tragically, starting in September 1944, almost 3,200 V-2s were fired on London and on Antwerp and Liège in Belgium. Between 5,000 and 9,000 people died in the attacks, and even more were wounded. Even worse, the Germans' Mittelwerk rocket factory was built using slave labor from the nearby Dora concentration camp. An estimated 12,000 prisoners were worked or starved to death to build the V-2s.

At the end of the war, von Braun and most of his engineers were captured and brought to the United States to develop missiles for the US Army. None of the German rocket scientists were ever prosecuted for war crimes. The United States and the Soviet Union were locked in the Cold War, and military and government leaders chose to ignore their dreadful history.

Sputnik Shock

On October 4, 1957, the Soviet Union announced that it had launched the world's first satellite, Sputnik 1. It was small and round, just 23 inches in diameter, and weighed 184 pounds. It did little more than broadcast a beeping radio signal as it circled the Earth.

Sputnik passed twice over the United States before the Americans realized it was up there. Once America found out, there was an uproar. *The Russians have beaten us to space! How could this happen?* If Americans wanted proof, they could go outside and scan the night sky. Every 96 minutes a tiny bright dot passed over.

Sergei Korolev, leader of the Soviet space program, was thrilled. "Well, comrades, you can't

It *Is* Rocket Science

How does a rocket work? This activity will demonstrate how the gas shooting from an "engine" pushes a rocket in the opposite direction.

YOU'LL NEED

🌙 String

🌙 Drinking straw

🌙 2 chairs

🌙 Balloon

🌙 Small binder clip

🌙 Tape

1. Cut an 8-to-10-foot length of string and a 3-inch piece of drinking straw.

2. Thread the string through the straw.

3. Tie the string between two chairs, then move the chairs apart until the string is tight.

4. Blow up a balloon—a sausage-shaped balloon works best—and clamp the opening with a binder clip.

5. Tape the balloon to the straw. Slide it to one end of the string, with the binder against one chair.

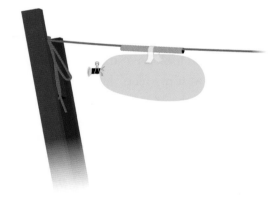

6. Quickly release the binder clip. What happens to the balloon?

imagine—the whole world is talking about our satellite," he said. "It seems like we have caused quite a stir."

President Dwight Eisenhower held a news conference five days later. Downplaying the Soviets' accomplishment, he announced that the United States planned to catch up to, and pass, their program.

But that wouldn't happen anytime soon. On November 2 the Russians launched Sputnik 2. It weighed 1,120 pounds and had dog named Laika aboard. Laika survived liftoff, but she overheated and died after a few hours in orbit.

Eisenhower ordered the army to get a satellite into space in 90 days or less. Von Braun was nearly ready with a new rocket, the Vanguard. On December 6 it was launched from Florida's Cape Canaveral on live TV. It rose four feet off the pad and exploded.

Finally, on January 31, 1958, von Braun successfully launched the Explorer 1 satellite atop a Juno rocket. A day later, it sent back proof of the Van Allen radiation belt surrounding Earth. It was a small victory.

On July 29, 1958, President Eisenhower signed the National Aeronautics and Space Act into law. "The Congress hereby declares that it is the policy of the United States that activities in space should be devoted to peaceful purposes for the benefit of all mankind," the act declared. It turned America's existing National Advisory Council for Astronautics (NACA) into the National Aeronautics and Space Agency—NASA.

Like NACA, NASA would be a civilian agency, even though several military operations—the army's Redstone Arsenal and the Naval Research Laboratory—were placed under its control. So were some research facilities, such as the Jet Propulsion Laboratory at the California Institute of Technology.

NASA began operations on October 1, 1958. A week later, Eisenhower approved Project Mercury. Its goal: to put the first human into space.

Project Mercury

On April 9, 1959, NASA introduced its first seven astronauts to the American people. Dr. Robert Voas, who had helped select them from 110 military test pilots, explained what NASA wanted: "Intelligence without genius, knowledge without inflexibility . . . fear but not cowardice, bravery without foolhardiness . . . enjoying life without excess, humor without disproportion, and fast reflexes without panic in a crisis." That basically described the Mercury Seven.

Americans *loved* the new astronauts. *Life* magazine signed a contract to tell their families' stories, and readers couldn't get enough. However, it would be more than two years before any of them flew to space.

It took time to develop the rocket, capsule, and space suit for Mercury. The first capsule design had no windows, making the astronauts feel more like riders than pilots. The Seven demanded it be changed—they weren't "Spam in a can," they said.

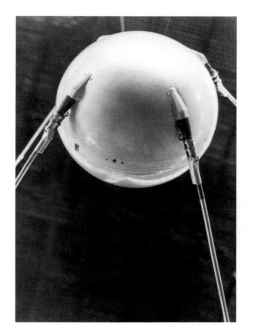

A mock-up of Sputnik 1.
Courtesy of NASA History Office

Moongazing

The largest features you can see on the moon—the light and dark patches, the mountains and craters—were given their names by Italian astronomer Giovanni Battista Riccioli in 1651. Though Riccioli used Latin, this book (like NASA) uses their English translations. See if you can identify the moon's features associated with the Apollo program.

YOU'LL NEED

- Telescope or binoculars
- Lunar map (www.lpi.usra.edu /resources/cla/)

1. First locate **Tycho**, the large white crater on the lunar map above. This will help you determine north and south. The full moon will appear to be lying on its left side if you look at it just after sundown, and on its right side just before sunrise. Also, if you look at the moon with a telescope, everything will be inverted—upside down—or mirrored left to right.

2. Turn your lunar map until it appears the same as what you see through your telescope or binoculars.

3. Locate the **Sea of Tranquility**, just east of the north-south axis at the equator. Apollo 11 landed here.

4. Find the **Ocean of Storms**. It is along the equator, *west* of the north-south axis. Apollo 12 landed here, and Apollo 14 landed just to the east at a spot called **Fra Mauro**.

5. Now locate the **Sea of Rains** and the **Sea of Serenity**. Apollo 15 landed in the **Apennine Mountains**—the white area between these two regions.

6. Refer to the photo to find the **Descartes Highlands**, southwest of the Sea of Tranquility. This is where Apollo 16 landed.

7. Finally, find **Taurus-Littrow**, where the Sea of Serenity meets the Sea of Tranquility. Apollo 17 landed here.

Bonus: View the moon when it is half full (called a quarter moon) along the terminator—the line separating the dark from the light. With a telescope you should see an uneven line. This jagged line shows the shadows cast by the moon's mountains, valleys, and craters.

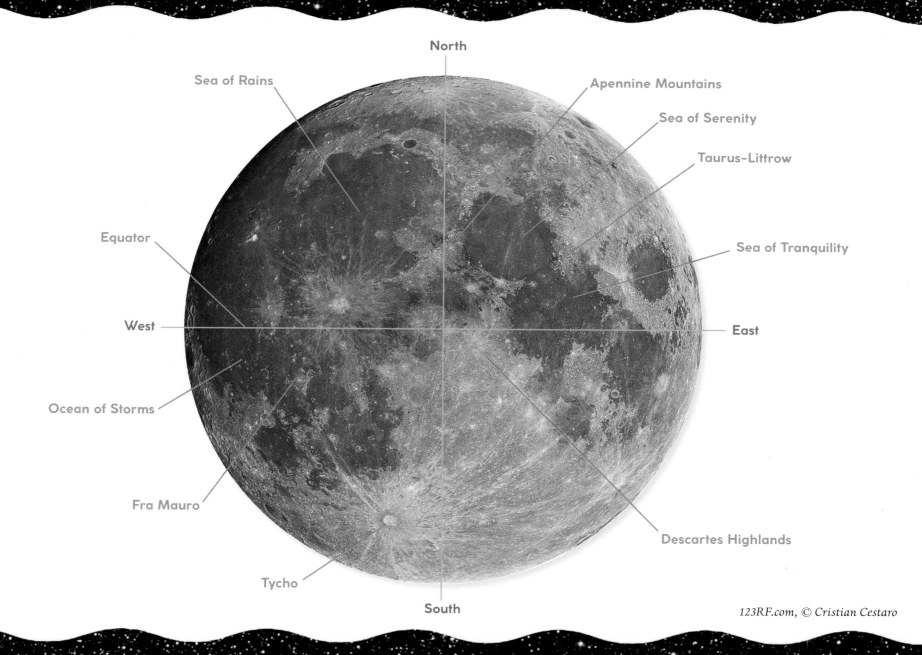

North

Sea of Rains

Apennine Mountains

Sea of Serenity

Taurus–Littrow

Equator

Sea of Tranquility

West

East

Ocean of Storms

Fra Mauro

Descartes Highlands

Tycho

South

123RF.com, © Cristian Cestaro

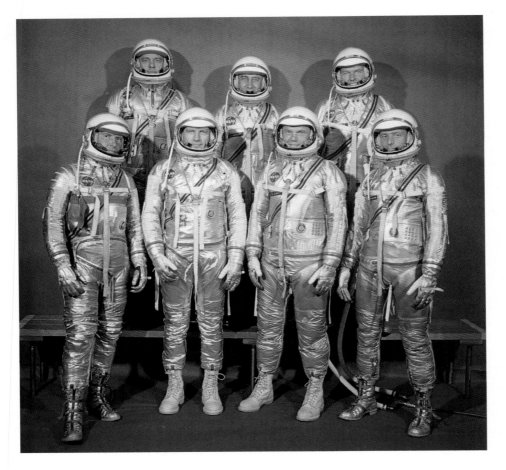

The Mercury Seven: (front, l to r) Wally Schirra, Deke Slayton, John Glenn, Scott Carpenter; (back, l to r) Alan Shepard, Gus Grissom, and Gordon Cooper. *Courtesy of NASA, S62-08774*

The rocket overshot its target by 124 miles and splashed down near Bermuda. Ham survived. Next it would be Alan Shepard's turn.

Then, on April 12, news arrived from Moscow that a 27-year-old cosmonaut named Yuri Gagarin had just orbited the Earth. Gagarin's Vostok 1 spacecraft had launched from the Baikonur Cosmodrome—the Soviets' launch facility—and 108 minutes later landed in a Russian farmer's field.

The Vostok was designed for Gagarin to eject before landing, then parachute the last couple miles. Two stunned women watched Gagarin and the capsule land in their field. "Don't be afraid!" he called out, still in his orange space suit. "I am a Soviet like you, who has descended from space, and I must find a telephone to call Moscow!"

On the other side of the globe, the Americans were just as surprised. The Russians had beaten them to space. Again. "We are behind," President Kennedy admitted. "The news will be worse before it is better, and it will be some time before we catch up."

Three weeks later, on May 5, Alan Shepard lifted off from Florida in his *Freedom 7* capsule. (The astronauts named their own spacecraft.) It was a quick flight, just over 15 minutes, but Shepard experienced 5 minutes of weightlessness. "Boy, what a ride!" Shepard said after making it safely back. "The only complaint I have was the flight was not long enough."

Gus Grissom flew the next Mercury mission on July 21. It was another quick flight like Shepard's, but it ran into trouble after splashing down. While he was waiting for a helicopter to lift him out of

And rather than have the spaceship be flown by controllers on the ground, they wanted to fly their capsules, or at least be able to take action if something went wrong. As test pilots, they knew something *always* went wrong.

In early 1961 NASA was almost ready. The first Mercury "astronaut" was a chimpanzee named Ham. On January 31, 1961, Ham rocketed 156.5 miles into space. During the 18-minute flight he pushed levers whenever lights flashed to show that he could think and move during the flight.

the ocean, the capsule's hatch blew off. Grissom jumped from the sinking spaceship and the *Liberty Bell 7* sank to the floor of the Atlantic.

The capsule's hatch was designed to explode off in an emergency. Many believed Grissom had panicked and pulled the escape lever, but he insisted he had not. That doubt would haunt the rest of his NASA career. But in 1999, long after Grissom had died, the capsule was raised from the ocean and inspected. He had been telling the truth.

NASA achieved its first orbital flight on February 20, 1962, when John Glenn circled the globe three times in *Friendship 7*. During the second orbit, Mission Control received data from a sensor that the capsule's heat shield might have come loose. If it were to come off during reentry, he would burn up in the atmosphere. Glenn was told to leave the capsule's retrorocket packet attached. It was strapped around the heat shield and normally would be detached before reentry. Maybe it would hold the heat shield in place.

Glenn made it back safely and was greeted as a hero. The mission made Glenn so popular that NASA wouldn't consider sending him on a second flight. (They eventually changed their minds, sending him on the Space Shuttle *Discovery* in October 1998. He was then 77 years old, the oldest person to ever fly to space.)

Deke Slayton was scheduled to take the next Mercury flight, but doctors discovered that he sometimes had an irregular heartbeat. He was pulled from the mission and was grounded by the air force as well. "I was just devastated," Slayton said.

NASA gave him a new job: director of flight crew operations. He was now responsible for deciding who would fly on every mission. This was one of the most important jobs at NASA, but everyone knew Slayton would trade it all for one trip to space.

Three more Mercury flights followed. On May 24, 1962, Scott Carpenter orbited the Earth three times in *Aurora 7*. Because of problems during reentry, he overshot the splashdown target by 250 miles. It took two hours to find him floating in the Atlantic near Puerto Rico.

John Glenn's *Friendship 7* launches from Pad 14, February 20, 1962. *Courtesy of NASA, 62PC-0011*

KATHERINE JOHNSON

Katherine Johnson was a computer. In the age before electronic computers were widely used, a computer was a person who performed complex mathematical calculations by hand. It was one of the few professional jobs at NASA that was open to women. Johnson was a math whiz and had earned a degree in mathematics (and French) from West Virginia State College at the age of 18.

Johnson was hired by NACA in 1953, before it became NASA. She worked at the Langley Memorial Aeronautical Laboratory in Hampton, Virginia, which was racially segregated at the time. This made her work even more difficult because Johnson was black.

Johnson's specialty was calculating flight trajectories—the paths rockets take into space and back. She sat in on engineering meetings, but unlike other computers, she spoke up. "The women did what they were told to do. They didn't ask questions or take the task any further," she recalled. "I asked questions; I wanted to know why. [The engineers] got used to me asking questions and being the only woman there."

Promoted to the Space Task Force in 1958, Johnson was both the only woman and only African American in the group. She would later be responsible for calculating the flight path on Alan Shepard's Mercury

mission. John Glenn insisted she do the same for his flight, rather than blindly trust NASA's new electronic computers. She later worked on the Apollo program, and received one of the small American flags that had gone to the moon on Apollo 11. In 2015 Johnson was awarded the Presidential Medal of Freedom.

Katherine Johnson. *Courtesy of NASA*

Later that year, on October 3, Wally Schirra flew six times around the Earth in *Sigma 7*. He landed in the Pacific less than five miles from the waiting USS *Kearsarge*.

Gordon Cooper piloted the final Mercury flight and spent more time in space than all the previous astronauts combined. *Faith 7* took off on May 15, 1963, on a 34-hour mission. During its final orbits the capsule started having electrical failures. Only Cooper's remarkable piloting skills saved the mission from disaster. And he splashed down closer to the recovery ship than any of the previous flights had.

Project Mercury had been a remarkable success. But the Soviet Union continued to pile up accomplishments. On August 11, 1962, cosmonaut Andriyan Nikolayev took off in Vostok 3. The next day, Pavel Popovich did the same in another rocket. At one point their capsules orbited within three miles of each other. And on June 16, 1963, Valentina Tereshkova became the first woman in space during a three-day mission aboard Vostok 6.

A Plan Takes Shape

Project Mercury taught NASA how to build a spacecraft and launch it into Earth orbit. But President Kennedy wanted to go to the *moon*.

There were several theories on how to get there. The most popular idea was called "Earth orbit rendezvous." Small rockets would carry parts of the Apollo spacecraft—whatever that turned out to be—into orbit around the Earth.

Once there, they would rendezvous (meet up), and crews would put the pieces together. After the spacecraft was assembled, it would fly to the moon and back. Wernher von Braun liked this plan.

But there was another idea called "lunar orbit rendezvous." It was suggested by NASA engineer John Houbolt. Two small spacecraft would be launched together into Earth orbit, then continue on to the moon. Once in lunar orbit, one ship would drop down to the surface and land. The other, holding enough fuel to return to Earth, would wait in lunar orbit. The lander would later

HANGAR RATS AND JUNIOR ASTRONAUTS

Most of America's first astronauts were born in the 1920s and '30s during the Golden Age of Aviation. For many, it sparked their interest in flying at an early age. Some even had pilots as parents.

"Mother and Dad barnstormed after World War I," recalled Wally Schirra. "Dad convinced mother to get out on the wing and act like a wing-walker." Ed White, whose father was a military pilot, gave Ed his first ride in a T-6 aircraft, and briefly let the six-year-old take the controls. "[It was] the most natural thing in the world to do," White said.

In 1936, just before he turned six, Neil Armstrong's parents allowed him to skip Sunday school for an early morning flight at a small airport in Warren, Ohio. Soon he was building model airplanes and reading everything he could about aviation. As a teen he worked after-school jobs to pay for flying lessons. The day he turned 16 he earned his pilot's license, though he had not yet learned how to drive a car.

Some future astronauts—Alan Shepard, Pete Conrad, Edgar Mitchell, and Tom Stafford—would hang out at local airports to wash planes, run errands, and hope to convince a pilot to take them up for a ride. "Hangar rats," some called them. "I had my first ride in an airplane—a lady instructor, a Taylorcraft [airplane], when I was 15 or 16, at the local airport, which was a grass strip," said Stafford.

Others set their sights even higher. As a child, Jim Lovell read Jules Verne's novels and became obsessed with rocketry and space. As a teen he built model rockets he designed himself, some three feet tall. Blanch Lovell, Jim's widowed mother, supported her son's hobby by helping him buy the gunpowder he needed for the engines. She would watch his experiments from their Milwaukee apartment as he shot off missiles from a vacant lot across the street. Many just exploded.

Though he didn't build rockets, Mike Collins dreamed of going to Mars or the Caverns of Mongo, like Flash Gordon did in the sci-fi movies he watched each Saturday. Alan Bean loved dime novels about space traveler Buck Rogers.

And Rusty Schweickart came up with his own dreams. "I lived in the country, on a farm, and my parents and I would walk on summer evenings. . . . I must have been five. . . . It was a full moon and fairly low in the sky, early evening, and I remember watching it go through the limbs of the trees," he recalled. He told his parents, "I'd like to go there one day." They chuckled at the idea.

NASA engineer John Houbolt explains lunar orbit rendezvous, July 24, 1962. *Courtesy of NASA, L-1962-05848*

the summer of 1962 NASA decided to go with Houbolt's plan.

North American Aviation, a company in Downey, California, was hired to build Apollo's command module (CM)—the main ship that would carry the astronauts to the moon and back. The lunar module (LM)—the lander—would be built by Grumman Aircraft on Long Island, New York. And the enormous rocket, known as the Saturn V, was constructed in pieces around the United States, then assembled at NASA's Launch Operations Center (LOC) in Florida.

The LOC began as a missile base for the US Air Force. Project Mercury flights took off from here, but Apollo needed something bigger. Much bigger. In 1962 NASA bought Merritt Island to the north, adding 87,763 acres just for Apollo. Each Saturn V would be put together inside a new 40-story building called the Vehicle Assembly Building (VAB). Once ready, the Saturn V would be slowly moved three and a half miles to the new launchpad (called Complex 39) atop a huge vehicle called the crawler-transporter, the largest self-powered land vehicle in the world.

All of this was just to *launch* the Apollo rockets. NASA also needed to build a new Mission Control facility to track the flights to the moon and back. Vice President Lyndon Johnson was from Texas, so it was no surprise when NASA chose Houston as the site for its Manned Spaceflight Center (MSC).

On September 12, 1962, President Kennedy spoke at Rice University for the MSC's dedication. (Rice had donated the land.) "The exploration of space will go ahead . . . and it is one of the great

blast off from the moon and rendezvous with the orbiting ship. The crew would then dump the lander and fly home.

"It occurred to me then that rendezvous around the moon was like being in a living room," Houbolt said. "Why take the whole darn living room down to the surface when it is easier to go down in a little tiny craft?" In early 1962, he presented the idea to several Apollo leaders.

"Your figures lie!" shouted Maxime Faget, who had designed the Mercury capsule.

Von Braun shook his head. "No, that's no good," he said, and rejected the plan.

But Houbolt didn't give up. He sent 100 copies of his report to anyone who would listen. Soon others were debating his idea, and agreeing. In

adventures of all time, and no nation which expects to be the leader of other nations can expect to stay behind in the race for space," he said, drawing parallels to other historic challenges. "We choose to go to the moon! We choose to go to the moon in this decade and do the other things—not because they are easy but because they are *hard*. . . . To be sure, we are behind, and we will be behind for some time in manned flight. But we do not intend to stay behind, and in this decade, we shall make up and move ahead."

Togethersville

NASA also needed more astronauts—a lot more than the seven they had. Less than a week after Kennedy's visit to Houston, nine more astronauts were introduced to the American public. A year later, another fourteen were added. There would be more, but most of the early Apollo astronauts came from these first three groups.

As the MSC was being built, so were the nearby communities of El Lago, Nassau Bay, Timber Cove, and Clear Lake City. Almost everyone who moved in worked for NASA. Reporters nicknamed the neighborhoods Togethersville.

"Everybody was working on a very exciting, challenging project. Everybody had one goal in mind: that was to eventually send man to the moon," recalled Jan Evans, wife of astronaut Ron Evans. "That was in a day and age when most women were stay-at-home mothers. The fathers of the families were all gone a great deal of the time, and yet they had very strong wives and families

who could function without them and look forward to when they would be back. Everybody just bound together."

As Apollo progressed, Togethersville became a tourist attraction. Buses loaded with sightseers would drive through the suburban streets looking for astronauts. Sometimes they would spot them mowing their lawns or fixing their cars.

Most of those working at NASA, however, were not headed to space. They were engineers and technicians, janitors and clerks, accountants and scientists. And they were all dedicated to achieving President Kennedy's goal.

"You could stand across the street [from the MSC] and you could not tell when quitting time was, because people didn't leave at quitting time in those days," recalled Neil Armstrong. "People just worked, and they worked until whatever their job was done, and if they had to be there until five o'clock or seven o'clock or nine-thirty or whatever it was, they were just there. They did it, and then they went home."

NASA was just beginning to put together the pieces of the moon puzzle when President Kennedy returned to Houston for a banquet on November 21, 1963. The following day, while riding in a motorcade through Dallas, Kennedy was assassinated.

The young president, who had set the bold goal of landing on the moon, was now dead. The nation was in shock. One week later the new president, Lyndon Johnson, renamed the Launch Operations Center in Florida. It would now be the John F. Kennedy Space Center.

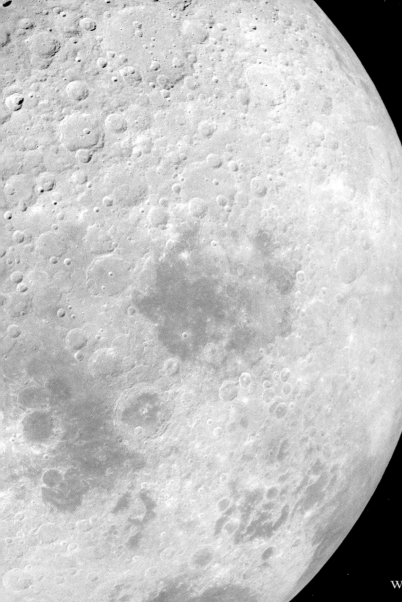

Project Gemini

On June 3, 1965, while passing over Hawaii, astronaut Ed White opened the hatch on the Gemini 4 capsule and floated out into space. For a while he used a "zip gun" to move about. It shot out small bursts of oxygen gas to push him in the opposite direction. It didn't work very well, or for very long. Soon White was tumbling around.

Still inside the capsule, commander Jim McDivitt tried to snap photos of White.

"It's just tremendous!" White said. "Right now I'm standing on my head, and I'm looking right down, and it looks like we're coming up on the coast of California." Soon he floated up to McDivitt's window.

"Hey! You smeared up my windshield, you dirty dog!" McDivitt joked. Neither man seemed to be paying attention to the clock. The space walk was supposed to last 12 minutes but had gone longer. White needed to return to the capsule before it reached the Atlantic and passed into Earth's shadow.

Ed White floating outside the Gemini 4 capsule, June 3, 1965. *Courtesy of NASA, S65-30427*

Down at Mission Control, Gus Grissom was trying to radio the astronauts. "Gemini 4, Houston," he repeated several times. Neither astronaut heard him.

Finally, McDivitt realized his receiver was turned off, and switched it back on. "Gus, this is Jim. Got any message for us?"

"Gemini 4, get back in!" Grissom barked.

McDivitt called to White, "They want you to come back in now."

"Back in?" asked White.

"Back in."

"Coming in," replied White. But not very fast—White kept taking photos as he inched toward the hatch.

McDivitt now sounded like a parent at bedtime. "Ed, come on in here! . . . Come on, let's get back here before it gets dark."

"OK," said White. "This is the saddest moment of my life."

Two at a Time

Before NASA could even think of sending anyone to the moon, it had to solve many difficult problems. Could astronauts survive being weightless for 10 days? How would two spacecraft maneuver to meet up in space, and could they dock once they did? Would it even be possible for an astronaut to leave the spacecraft and "walk" in zero gravity, or on the moon's surface? And navigation—could Apollo even find its way to the moon, orbit for a few days, and return to Earth?

Project Gemini was designed to answer those questions and more, and to train astronauts for trips to the moon. Each Gemini flight would have two crew members—a commander and a pilot—and each flight would build on the previous missions.

While the engineers designed and built the Gemini spacecraft, the astronauts trained on Earth. To see if the astronauts could survive liftoff and reentry through the atmosphere, they were placed in a machine called a centrifuge. Standing on the ground, everyone feels 1 G, which is

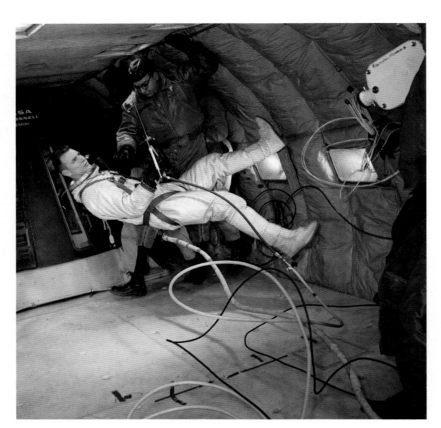

Dave Scott floats in the Vomit Comet during Gemini 8 training, February 3, 1966. *Courtesy of NASA, S66-20016*

shorthand for saying "the gravitational pull felt on the Earth's surface." But if you get on a spinning amusement park ride, you will feel heavier the faster it spins. If you feel 2 Gs, you feel twice as heavy. NASA's centrifuge could spin astronauts so fast they would feel 15 times heavier. Engineers didn't expect them to experience that during a flight, but it was good training for the 7 and 8 Gs they would feel during takeoff and reentry.

During most of the flights, however, they would experience 0 Gs—weightlessness. There is no way to turn off Earth's gravity, but an airplane pilot can create the sensation by flying in an arched path, like a ball thrown through the air. For 20 to 25 seconds everyone inside the plane will feel weightless as they "fall" through the sky.

NASA designed a KC-135A tanker plane for this purpose. It was hollow inside and its walls were padded to keep passengers from injuring themselves as they floated around. During a single flight, the plane would make 50 to 60 arching dives as the astronauts practiced tasks they would need to perform in space. Most on board got airsick and called the plane the Vomit Comet.

If the zero-gravity training didn't make the astronauts sick, their survival training might. The Gemini flights would pass over land as well as water, and the astronauts had to be prepared if they came down in a desert or jungle. They spent two weeks in the Panama rainforest, where a survival guide said, "Anything that creeps, crawls, swims, or flies is a possible source of food." Iguanas, rats, snakes, snails, taro root, and heart of palm—all were on the menu.

Desert training was done near Reno, Nevada. Here they learned to make lightweight clothing from Gemini parachutes. (You wouldn't want to hike through a blistering desert in a 30-pound space suit.)

After making it through training, astronauts were given a silver pin of a star rising into orbit. If they ever made it to space, they would receive a gold pin.

Astronauts (l to r) Frank Borman, Neil Armstrong, John Young, and Deke Slayton during survival training in Nevada, August 3, 1964. *Courtesy of NASA, S64-145074*

Shooting at the Moon

One of the most difficult challenges for a moon landing was getting to the moon in the first place. It wasn't as simple as firing a rocket at it.

Once again, the Soviet Union had beaten the United States. In early January 1959 they launched the Luna 1 probe at the moon, but missed it by 3,700 miles. Luna 2 crashed into the moon's Sea of Rains on September 13, 1959. Then, on October 7, Luna 3 swung around the moon and transmitted back 17 photos. This was the first time anyone had seen its far side.

Meanwhile, NASA was shooting its own spacecraft at the moon, but with less success. The Ranger program was designed to fly spacecraft directly at the moon and send back live TV footage until they crashed into it.

The first six Rangers failed. Two didn't make it out of Earth orbit, two missed the moon entirely, and two hit the surface but didn't send back any pictures. Finally, on July 31, 1964, Ranger 7 transmitted 4,308 photos of oncoming craters before slamming into the Sea of Clouds. Two successful Ranger missions followed in 1965.

At this time, the Soviets were trying to make a "soft" landing on the moon. Lunas 4, 5, 6, 7, and 8 all failed. But on February 3, 1966, Luna 9 touched down on the Ocean of Storms. It sent back 27 photos from the surface.

The first up-close photo of the moon's surface, taken by Luna 9, February 3, 1966.
Courtesy of Wikimedia Commons

Just four months later, on June 2, NASA successfully landed Surveyor 1 on the moon. It took 11,150 black-and-white TV photos of the surface. Six more Surveyors followed—two crashed and four survived, sending back important data for Apollo planners. Surveyor 3 dug four small trenches in the lunar soil to see if it could support the weight of a large spacecraft. (Some at NASA worried the Apollo lander would sink into a thick layer of powdery dust.)

NASA also surveyed the moon from above. It sent five Lunar Orbiters, from August 1966 to August 1967, which sent a total of 1,950 photos of possible Apollo landing sites.

Saturn V

Sending a small space probe to the moon was difficult enough. For Apollo, which would be much heavier, NASA needed a big rocket, bigger than anyone had ever created. Fortunately, Wernher von Braun had a head start.

Since 1950, von Braun had been working at the US Army's Redstone Arsenal in Huntsville, Alabama, building larger and larger rockets. The arsenal was made part of NASA in 1960, when it was renamed the Marshall Space Flight Center (MSFC). Von Braun was named its director.

Before Sputnik, von Braun had worked on a series of military rockets named Jupiter. One of those modified rockets, called Juno, launched America's first satellite—Explorer 1. He named the next (larger) series of rockets after another Roman god: Saturn.

The Face of the Moon

When you look at the moon, have you ever wondered why the features you see always look the same? The shadow changes as it goes from crescent moon to full, then back, but the face you see remains the same. Why don't you ever see its far side?

YOU'LL NEED

🌙 Chair

🌙 Globe (optional)

1. Place a chair in the middle of an open space. If you have a globe, place it on the chair. In this activity, the chair/globe is the Earth. You will be the moon.

2. Step away from the chair several feet, still facing the chair.

3. The moon orbits the Earth counter-clockwise. Slowly move a quarter way around the chair, keeping your face pointed at the chair. Did your body have to turn?

4. Continue to move around the chair, always facing it, to the halfway point.

5. Look around you. Has your body changed direction? You should have turned halfway around as you moved halfway around the chair.

6. Continue to move counterclockwise around the chair, always facing it, until you reach your starting point. You've made one full orbit. How many times have you "revolved on your axis"?

Bonus: Now imagine you are standing on the surface of the moon. How would the Earth look from there? How would it change day by day?

Bonus answer: The Earth will always remain at the same place in the sky when viewed from the moon. It will also appear to go through light and dark phases, like the moon, and revolve on its axis once a day.

THE SATURN V

The Saturn V was the tallest and most powerful rocket ever constructed—and still holds both records to this day. It was a three-stage rocket. As soon as the fuel in each stage was used up, it separated from the rest of the rocket and the next stage ignited.

The Saturn V's **first stage**, called the S-IC, was 138 feet tall, 33 feet in diameter, and had five bell-shaped F-1 engines. Each engine was 18½ feet tall, and together they could generate 7.6 million pounds of thrust. That's about the same power as 60,000 minivans pulling together. The first stage burned kerosene and liquid oxygen (LOX), 15 tons every second, and its flame was 800 feet long. Once the Saturn V was 38 miles high, moving at 6,100 mph, the stage-one engine would break away and fall back through the atmosphere into the ocean.

The Saturn V's **second stage**, called the S-II, would then fire. This stage was 81 feet tall and its five J-2 engines burned a mixture of liquid hydrogen and oxygen. They would push the spacecraft to 109 miles above the Earth, moving at 15,300 mph.

Adapted from Apollo Logistics Training Manual *(North American Aviation, 1965), author's collection*

The **third stage**, known as the S-IVB, would fire after the second stage fell away. This stage was 59 feet tall and had a single J-2 engine. It would boost the rocket to 17,400 mph where it would "park" in orbit around the Earth, 118 miles high. However, this stage remained attached, because it would be fired several hours later to push the spacecraft out of Earth orbit on a path to the moon, going 24,000 mph.

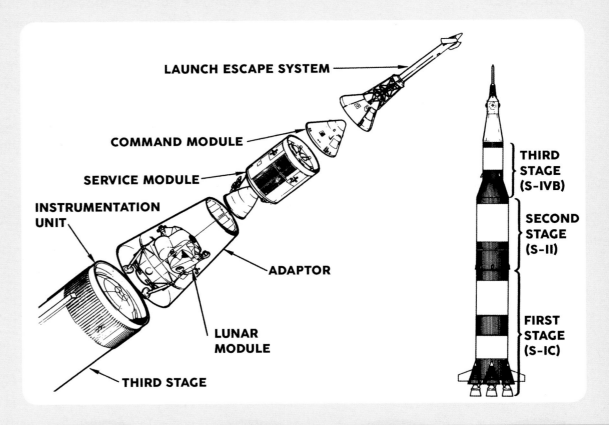

LAUNCH ESCAPE SYSTEM

COMMAND MODULE

SERVICE MODULE

INSTRUMENTATION UNIT

ADAPTOR

LUNAR MODULE

THIRD STAGE

THIRD STAGE (S-IVB)

SECOND STAGE (S-II)

FIRST STAGE (S-IC)

Just above the third stage was a 3-foot-tall ring called the **instrumentation unit**. It held most of the electronics that controlled and guided the rocket.

The astronauts rode the Saturn V inside the **command module**, or CM, which was attached to the **service module** (SM) for most of the mission. Together they were called the command and service module (CSM). (See page 58 for more details.) Behind the CSM was a cone-shaped **adaptor** that protected the **lunar module** (LM), the four-legged spacecraft that would land on the moon. (See page 68.)

Finally, the Saturn V was topped with a **launch escape system**. In an emergency, the 33-foot tower would fire its powerful internal rocket to pull the CM away from the Saturn V. If it survived, the CM would then parachute back to Earth with its crew. Luckily, it never had to be used—the Saturn V flew 13 times and never failed.

When it launched, the Saturn V and its crew and cargo weighed 6,500,000 pounds. When the CM returned to Earth, only 11,000 pounds remained—the rest had burned up or had been left behind.

There were many different Saturn designs, all made with different engines and parts from earlier US rockets. This made the development and testing easier because the engineers knew how the pieces worked. Only three versions would ever be built. The Saturn 1 was used only for unmanned flights. The Saturn 1B, a modified Saturn 1, sent Apollo spacecraft into Earth orbit, but no farther. And the much larger Saturn V (V being the Roman numeral for 5) launched Apollo to the moon.

But first it had to be built. Von Braun favored a careful approach with many launches. Each flight would test a new piece of the proposed final rocket. This would take time, and time was something Apollo didn't have much of. So in 1963 NASA administrator George Mueller decided the Saturn V would go through "all-up testing," meaning many different systems would be tested on a single flight. If the rocket's first stage failed, the second and third stages would be destroyed,

There were five massive F-1 engines on the Saturn V's first stage. Two technicians stand in front. *Courtesy of NASA, RD-ENG-634*

How Big Was the Saturn V?

The Saturn V was enormous—363 feet tall! To get a sense of how big that is, walk the length of a football field, which is 360 feet long including end zones.

YOU'LL NEED

- 6 distance markers—flags, bright towels, etc.
- Football field

1. Contact your local high school to get permission to use its football field for this activity.

2. Start in one end zone. Walk toward the other end zone until you reach the 36-yard line. Mark the point with a flag or bright towel laid on the field. This distance—138 feet—is the length of the Saturn V's **first stage**.

3. Walk in the same direction, past the 50-yard line, to the 37-yard line and mark the spot with another flag or towel. This distance—81 feet—is the length of the **second stage**.

4. Walk to the 17-yard line and place a marker. This is the length of the **third stage**—59 feet.

5. Take one large step, just 1 yard, and mark it. This was the height of the **instrumentation unit**.

6. Now walk to the 5-yard line, just 32 feet, and mark it. Apollo's **lunar module** (LM) fit here, inside the rocket's cone-shaped adaptor.

7. Walk halfway into the end zone and mark it. This is the length of the **command and service module** (CSM). The astronauts rode into space in the CSM.

8. The final distance, to the back line in the end zone and one yard more, was the **escape tower**, the pointed tip of the rocket.

Bonus: If you live near a city with tall buildings, investigate whether you can visit one and ride to the 36th floor. Look out a window—this is approximately how tall the Saturn V was.

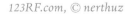

123RF.com, © nerthuz

along with any spacecraft the rocket was carrying. However, if the first stage worked, and then the second stage, and the third, the program just might meet Kennedy's end-of-decade challenge. It was a bold and risky idea.

First Flights

The first two Gemini flights were unmanned. Gemini 1 took off on April 8, 1964. Engineers followed the spacecraft (not much more than an empty shell) for almost five hours as it made three orbits of the Earth. Four days later the capsule tumbled back through the atmosphere and burned up.

Technical problems and three hurricanes delayed the launch of Gemini 2. Meanwhile, on October 12, the Soviets launched Voskhod 1. Vladimir Komarov, Boris Yegorov, and Konstantin Feoktistov orbited the Earth 17 times and returned a day later. The three-man flight was meant to embarrass the Americans, who had yet to launch a two-man crew. And it did. Yet the cosmonauts had flown without their bulky space suits—there wasn't enough room in the capsule. NASA would have been less impressed had it known the Soviets were needlessly endangering the crew.

Three months later, on January 19, 1965, Gemini 2 rose into the Florida sky for a quick, 18-minute test flight. The rocket and capsule performed (mostly) as planned.

Now it was time for the first manned mission. Gus Grissom and John Young had trained together for almost two years. On March 23, the Titan rocket roared off Pad 19 and was soon in orbit.

Once Mission Control confirmed that Gemini 3 was working properly, Grissom was told to fire its maneuvering thrusters. The spacecraft had been flying in an elliptical (oval) orbit. Grissom changed it to a circular one—the first time this had been done by an astronaut in orbit.

Two hours into the flight, John Young was scheduled to test NASA's new food packets. Instead, he reached into his space suit and pulled out a paper-wrapped bundle. It was a corned beef sandwich he had smuggled aboard as a joke. Both men took a bite and crumbs floated everywhere. Grissom complained that it didn't have mustard.

Gemini 3 continued on for another three hours and returned to Earth after its third orbit. The reentry was guided by an onboard computer, which could make 7,000 calculations each second—another first for NASA. When its parachutes opened, the jolt flung the astronauts into the control panel, puncturing Grissom's faceplate.

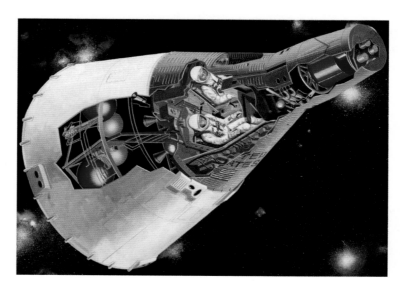

An artist's rendering of the Gemini capsule. *Courtesy of NASA, S65-14257*

After splashing down, the capsule was dragged underwater by its parachutes. Once released, the spacecraft bobbed upright. But Grissom wasn't taking any chances on another sunken capsule—he kept the hatches closed until divers attached a flotation collar. Then, after removing their space suits, the men were hoisted into a helicopter in their long underwear.

Gemini 3 was the last NASA mission controlled from Florida. Though flights still would launch from Kennedy Space Center, future missions would be controlled from the just-finished Manned Spacecraft Center (MSC) in Houston. And the next flight was just 10 weeks away.

Extravehicular Activity

Though many say "space walk" or "moonwalk" to describe when an astronaut leaves a spacecraft, NASA prefers "extravehicular activity," or just EVA (pronounced ee-vee-ay). If humans ever hoped to explore space, they would have to leave their capsules—to make repairs, to perform experiments, to gather rock and soil samples. Gemini 4's main goal was to perform the first EVA.

And the Soviets beat the Americans again. On March 18, 1965, cosmonaut Alexei Leonov floated outside the Voskhod 2 spacecraft for 20 minutes while his crewmate, Pavel Belyayev, waited inside. Then when Leonov tried to return to the capsule, he couldn't. His space suit had expanded like a balloon and he couldn't fit. Only after he opened a valve on the suit to lower the pressure did he shrink enough to close the hatch.

For Gemini 4's EVA, astronaut Ed White was going to open the hatch and stand up, halfway out of the capsule. Nothing more. But after Voskhod 2, the plan changed. Now White would leave the capsule entirely, connected only by a 23-foot umbilical line that pumped oxygen into his suit.

Gemini 4 launched on June 3, 1965, with Jim McDivitt as commander and Ed White as pilot. On its third orbit, White opened the hatch and stepped out.

The EVA did not go as planned. White had trouble maneuvering, and before long he was drifting around. And because he was connected to the capsule, the spacecraft turned too. "When Ed gets out there and starts wiggling around, it sure

Ed White during the Gemini 4 EVA, June 3, 1965. *Courtesy of NASA, S65-29766*

makes the spacecraft tough to control," McDivitt reported.

Still, White was enjoying himself. "When the order came to go back in, I did feel certain sadness," he admitted. "There was so much out there I wanted to learn."

Getting back in wasn't easy. Tangled in the long umbilical line, the pair had trouble closing the hatch. McDivitt wiggled the latch with his finger while White pulled the hatch with all his strength. At last, it worked.

Gemini 4 orbited for four more days. The pair performed medical experiments, measured the radiation inside and outside the capsule, and photographed the Earth.

The spacecraft's computer failed near the end of the mission, but the ship returned safely. It reentered the atmosphere over Mexico and splashed down in the North Atlantic. "We hit the water and we checked around for leaks," McDivitt remembered, "and I said to Ed, 'How are you feeling?' He says, 'I'm feeling great. How are you feeling?' 'I'm feeling great, too. Guess we aren't going to die!'"

Eight Days in a Garbage Can

Gemini 5 was a test of human endurance. Could astronauts function in space for eight days, the time it would take to travel to the moon and back? Mercury veteran Gordon Cooper was chosen to command the mission and Pete Conrad would be the pilot. They would fly an improved Gemini capsule, one that used fuel cells for its power rather than heavy batteries.

Gemini 5 launched on August 21, 1965, and had problems almost immediately—one of the fuel cells began to fail. The astronauts had just released a pod into orbit so they could practice rendezvousing with it, but it drifted off and was lost while they were trying to fix the fuel cell. Just before Mission Control called an early end to the flight, the fuel cell mysteriously recovered.

Over the next few days, other systems failed. The astronauts had to power down the capsule and only use its dwindling electricity for essential functions. With little to do, they drifted in and out of the sunlight as they orbited the planet. Empty food containers filled the cabin—Conrad called it a "floating garbage can." With the astronauts barely able to move, their legs cramped up.

Back in Houston, the astronauts' families were told when to watch for the capsule. One morning at 5:00 AM, they gathered on the Coopers' front lawn to follow a tiny bright dot as it passed through the night sky over their heads.

"Isn't it gorgeous? Isn't it marvelous?" Trudy Cooper asked, her two daughters by her side.

Jane Conrad sat in the middle of her quiet, empty street to get the best view. "When I saw him up there he was like a star. Sitting there looking up at him was the first time it hit me—Pete was really up there, out of this world," she said.

After nearly eight days, Gemini 5 splashed down in the Atlantic. The Conrads' sons celebrated with their own splashdowns for a crowd of reporters back in Houston. Tommy rode his bike

into the family pool, and Christopher jumped off the roof into the water.

Rendezvous

On October 25, 1965, an Agena Target Vehicle—a "dummy" spacecraft—launched from Kennedy Space Center. Six minutes later it exploded. Back on the ground, Wally Schirra and Tom Stafford were already strapped into their Gemini 6 capsule,

ready for liftoff. The plan was to chase the Agena into orbit and join it: rendezvous. But not now.

A new plan quickly emerged. Rather than rendezvous with another Agena, Gemini 6 would meet up with Gemini 7, which was scheduled to launch in December. Gemini 7 was going to be another endurance mission—this time for two weeks. Now its crew would get visitors.

Gemini 7 took off on December 4. Commander Frank Borman and pilot Jim Lovell each brought a paperback book in case they got bored, but neither had much time to read. Instead, they performed experiments.

Then, on December 12, Gemini 6 was ready to go. As the countdown reached zero, the engines fired for 1.2 seconds, then stopped. A plug had disconnected from the rocket, shutting down the engines. Luckily Schirra, an experienced test pilot, did not pull the abort handle, which would have ejected the men from the capsule. The rocket was undamaged, and three days later was ready for another try.

From orbit, Borman and Lovell could see the launch. "It was a real high point to see this bright light—it looked like a star—came up, and then eventually we could see it was a Gemini vehicle," Borman remembered.

"It will be getting crowded up here," said Lovell. Six hours later, it was. Gemini 6 was able to maneuver within feet of Gemini 7. For three orbits, the two spacecraft floated around each other.

Near the end of the rendezvous, Tom Stafford radioed a startled Mission Control that Gemini 6 had spotted *another* spacecraft. "We have an object, looks like a satellite, going from north to south, up in a polar orbit," he said. "Stand by . . . it looks like it's trying to signal us."

A harmonica was heard over the radio. It was playing "Jingle Bells," followed by the sound of sleigh bells. Christmas was 10 days away—it was all a prank.

Gemini 6 returned the next day. It splashed down in the Atlantic and was recovered by the USS *Wasp*. Two days later, on December 18, Gemini 7 returned and was met by the same ship. Borman and Lovell had been in space for nearly 14 days—a record they would hold for eight years.

Docking

NASA lost its first astronauts during Gemini, but not during spaceflights. On October 31, 1964, Ted Freeman was killed when his T-38 jet struck a goose and crashed. Then, 16 months later, Elliot See and Charlie Bassett died when their plane went down during a snowstorm. The backup crew was given their assignments, and the program marched on.

After showing that two Gemini capsules could rendezvous, it was time for NASA to attempt docking. The plan for Gemini 8 was to dock with an Agena Target Vehicle four times during a three-day mission. Neil Armstrong was picked to command the flight, with Dave Scott as pilot.

Gemini 8 lifted off on March 16, 1966. In just over six hours it rendezvoused with the Agena. As both orbited at 17,500 mph, Armstrong guided the capsule toward the Agena at just inches per second.

"Flight, we are docked," Armstrong finally reported. "Yes, it's a real smoothie."

But it wasn't smooth for long. Scott noticed that the linked spacecraft were slowly beginning to tilt sideways. Armstrong tried to correct the problem, but couldn't. He thought it was caused by the Agena, so he undocked.

But it wasn't the Agena. Once free, the Gemini capsule began spinning, faster and faster and faster.

"We have serious problems, here," Scott reported to Mission Control. "We're . . . we're

Gemini 7, as seen from Gemini 6, during NASA's first rendezvous, December 15, 1965. *Courtesy of NASA, S65-63194*

Orbital Mechanics Made Easy

When a spacecraft orbits the Earth, the farther away it is from the planet the slower it moves. Most Apollo spaceflights orbited at 1,200 miles above the Earth's surface at 17,500 mph. Some satellites orbit 35,800 miles out at a speed of 6,900 mph. The moon, which is 240,000 miles away, orbits the Earth at the "slow" speed of 2,300 mph.

You can see this for yourself by doing an experiment in your kitchen.

YOU'LL NEED

- Large shallow bowl (or metal wok)
- Marble

1. Check with an adult to make sure it is OK to use the bowl you choose.
2. Place the marble in the bowl. Use your hands to gently swirl the bowl in a circle so that the marble rolls in orbit near the bottom of the bowl, close to the center. Observe how fast it moves.
3. Now swirl the bowl a little harder, so that the marble orbits near the top edge. (This might take some practice.) How fast does it move this time? Is it faster or slower than the lower orbit?

tumbling end over end up here." And then the radio signal went dead.

One of the Gemini's maneuvering thrusters had short-circuited and kept firing. Soon the spacecraft was whirling once every second, which caused the crew's vision to blur. Armstrong shut off the thrusters and used a second set to regain control.

Now the mission had to be scrubbed. Armstrong had fired Gemini's reentry thrusters, which were used to guide the capsule back through the atmosphere. Gemini 8 would have to return immediately.

"It was a great disappointment to us, to have to cut that flight short," Armstrong said later. "We had so many things we wanted to do."

Gemini 8 wasn't a complete loss. The astronauts had successfully docked—the first time that had ever been done, including by the Soviets. NASA had also been able to test its emergency procedures with a real emergency. And most important, Armstrong had demonstrated he could remain cool in the face of near-certain disaster.

Five days after Gemini 8, NASA announced the crew for the first Apollo mission, scheduled to launch in early 1967. Gus Grissom would be commander. Ed White, the first American to "walk" in space, and rookie Roger Chaffee rounded out the crew.

The Angry Alligator

There were still four more Gemini missions planned for 1966. Gemini 9 would practice docking with an unmanned spacecraft called the augmented target docking adaptor, or ATDA. The ATDA was launched on June 1, and two days later Tom Stafford and Gene Cernan lifted off on a three-day mission, chasing it.

When Gemini 9 reached the ATDA, the astronauts found its nose cone was still attached. Kind of. The nose was supposed to break in half and float away after launch, but a strap had tangled around the two pieces.

"The jaws are like an alligator's jaws that's open at 25 or 30 degrees. . . . Looks like an angry alligator out here rotating around," reported Stafford.

Mission Control wondered if Cernan could use his EVA to free the pieces instead. "They wanted him to go out and cut loose the shroud," Stafford said later. "I looked at it. I could see those sharp edges. We had never practiced that. I knew that they had those 300-pound springs there, didn't know what else. So I vetoed it right there. I said, 'No way.'"

Instead, the crew practiced rendezvousing with the crippled ATDA. Twice they moved miles away from the spacecraft, then returned to orbit beside it.

On the second day, it was time for Cernan's space walk. He immediately had problems. When pressurized, Cernan's space suit was stiff and hard to move, and the umbilical line floated all around. It was like wrestling an octopus while wearing a suit of armor.

Cernan was supposed to test an emergency life-support backpack—it could be used if the umbilical failed—as well as an astronaut maneuvering unit (AMU). The AMU was an improved

The "Angry Alligator," June 3, 1966. *Courtesy of NASA, S66-37966*

version of the zip gun Ed White had used. Both were stored in the back of the spacecraft. Cernan's first job outside was to crawl back and get them.

The Gemini capsule didn't have much to grab on to. Worse yet, there were razor-sharp edges where the rocket had detached from the capsule, edges that could slice through the umbilical or Cernan's space suit.

Cernan's heart raced as he struggled to work. Sweat from his body fogged up the inside of his visor and turned to ice. To see out, he pressed his nose against the visor to melt a small peephole. Finally, Stafford called off the EVA.

Both astronauts strained to get Cernan back inside the capsule. Crunched down by the hatch, Cernan pleaded, "Tom, if we aren't able to pressurize the ship quickly, I think I'm going to die here." Stafford pumped oxygen into the cabin and pulled Cernan's helmet off.

"His face was pink, like he'd been in a sauna," Stafford remembered. "He says, 'Help me get off my gloves, too.' . . . His hands were absolutely pink. So I took the water gun and just hosed him down [even though] you shouldn't squirt water around in a spacecraft." Cernan had sweat out 10½ pounds of water during the two-hour EVA.

The next day, Gemini 9 returned to Earth.

More Flights, More Practice

The following month, Gemini 10 took off. Less than six hours after launch, commander John Young and pilot Mike Collins docked with an

Agena. "John made it look easy. On the first try we glided right into the docking cone," Collins said.

Once linked, Young could control the Agena's engine and thrusters. Young fired the Agena's engine to push both spacecraft to a higher orbit where they would later rendezvous with *another* Agena, the one left behind by Gemini 8.

Before attempting the next rendezvous, the crew spent a day on experiments, and Collins performed an EVA. Gemini 10 rendezvoused with the second Agena the next day but didn't dock. Instead, on a second EVA, Collins launched himself out of the Gemini capsule toward the Agena. There, he grabbed an experiment left months earlier to see if it had collected any space microbes or micrometeorites. He then used an improved zip gun to propel himself back to Gemini. After another day running tests, Gemini 10 returned to Earth on July 21.

Eight weeks later, Gemini 11 was orbiting with commander Pete Conrad and pilot Dick Gordon. They started by chasing down an Agena. Conrad rendezvoused and docked before Gemini had completed its first orbit.

Once again, the EVA was difficult. Gordon had to attach a tether (a long cord) between the Agena and the Gemini capsule. Engineers had added a grab bar outside the capsule, but it didn't help much. With one hand on the grab bar, attaching the tether was like "trying to tie your shoelace with one hand," Gordon said.

Before launch, Deke Slayton and flight director Gene Kranz warned Conrad that he might have to leave Gordon behind if the EVA went wrong. And now it had—Gordon's visor fogged up, his heart raced, and his eyes burned. Conrad had to grab Gordon's feet to pull him back inside.

Later Conrad fired the Agena's engine to push the two docked spacecraft to a higher orbit. When they were 852 miles up, Conrad was awestruck. "The world's round!" he exclaimed. "I can see all the way from the end, around the top!"

Two hours later Gemini 11 returned to a lower orbit. The capsule then undocked from the Agena and backed away, still connected by the 100-foot tether. Carefully firing the Gemini's thrusters, Conrad got the two linked spacecraft to cartwheel around each other. Like the outward force riders feel on a merry-go-round, the astronauts in the spinning spacecraft should feel an "artificial gravity." The experiment did not go as expected, however—the tether whipped around like a jump rope. Gemini 11 returned to Earth the next day.

With one Gemini flight left, NASA was determined to solve the EVA problem. Astronaut Buzz Aldrin trained endlessly in an underwater tank— the first time this had been tried. Just as you feel lighter in a swimming pool, Aldrin felt "weightless" as he practiced on a mock-up of the capsule. Engineers added even more handholds and footholds to the spacecraft.

On November 11, 1966, commander Jim Lovell and Aldrin headed out to the launchpad. Lovell had a handwritten sign taped to his back that said THE and Aldrin had another that said END.

Gemini 12 was to rendezvous with an Agena, but when it was still 70 miles away its radar system failed. Aldrin, whom the other astronauts had nicknamed "Dr. Rendezvous," pulled out charts he'd brought along and calculated how to find the Agena without the computer. It worked, and they docked in record time.

Buzz Aldrin impressed everyone by performing three EVAs during the four-day mission, for a total of five and a half hours. He cut cables, turned bolts, hooked up plugs—tasks that would be needed during Apollo—and made it all look easy. Aldrin had joked earlier that it was like being a trained monkey. As a prank, somebody slipped a banana into his tool bag, which he didn't find until he was in space.

Gemini 12 returned on November 15 and splashed down in the Atlantic. A helicopter lifted the astronauts onto the deck of the USS *Wasp*, and Project Gemini came to an end.

Sixteen astronauts had flown during Gemini— four of them twice—logging 969 hours in space. They'd solved the problems of rendezvous, docking, EVAs, and much more. "By the time we came out of Gemini, we were a very tough, confident group of people," said Mission Control's Glynn Lunney. Yet the most difficult challenges were still to come.

Jim Lovell and Buzz Aldrin head for the final Gemini launch with signs on their backs, November 11, 1966. *Courtesy of NASA, KSC-66C-9220*

Tragedy and Triumph

On January 27, 1967, Pat White picked up her 10-year-old daughter, Bonnie, from ballet practice and headed back to their home in El Lago. Her husband Ed was away at Kennedy Space Center for another test of the Apollo spacecraft. As she pulled into the driveway, White found her neighbor Jan Armstrong waiting by the front door.

"There's been a problem," Armstrong said. "I don't know what it is." The women went inside. Soon the doorbell rang—it was Bill Anders.

Two other astronauts' families received similar visits that evening. Martha Chaffee was visited by neighbors Sue Bean, Clare Schweickart, and Barbara Cernan. "I thought you might like some company," Sue offered, but didn't say why.

Commander Gus Grissom enters the Apollo 1 capsule for a routine test, followed by Roger Chaffee and Ed White, October 18, 1966.
Courtesy of NASA, S66–58O38

Astronaut Mike Collins soon arrived. "Martha, I'd like to talk to you alone," Collins said, but his face said everything.

"Mike, I think I know, but I have to hear it," Chaffee replied.

In Timber Cove Jo Schirra went next door to Betty Grissom's house, coming through a break in the fence that connected their backyards. Another NASA neighbor, Adelin Hammack, was already there. "There's been an accident at the Cape. I think Gus was hurt," Schirra said.

Soon NASA's chief physician Chuck Berry arrived with the news. The entire crew of Apollo 1 was gone, killed in a fire on the pad.

"Go Fever"

Before that day NASA had been lucky. Though there had been many problems and accidents during the Mercury and Gemini flights, none of the 19 astronauts who'd flown had been seriously injured, much less killed. And for those who previously had been test pilots, launching into space almost seemed *safer* than flying an experimental new jet.

The space agency and its contractors were under tremendous pressure to keep on schedule if they were going to land on the moon before December 31, 1969. They wanted to keep President Kennedy's promise.

"And here it was, 1967. Time was getting short and [the] schedule was considered God," Walt Cunningham remembered. "So, anything that would slow things down, it was really tough to

get through. They didn't ignore it, but it just didn't have the same weight as it did before. The managers had 'go fever.'"

"Go fever." Astronauts who had been test pilots knew the term. You could be so determined to get a new plane in the air that you overlooked problems—even big problems. Apollo was no different. "We knew that it was bad, but we wanted to fly," said Cunningham. "We also had such big egos that we felt that we could fly the crates they shipped these things in."

In August 1966 the first Apollo capsule was moved from the California plant to Kennedy Space Center, even though more than 100 engineering changes had yet to be made to the spacecraft. Over the next five months, 623 other modifications were made to the capsule.

Looking back after the accident, it was clear that two of the biggest mistakes were made much earlier. First, the Apollo capsule had a complicated two-door hatch. One opened inward, and the other out. Gus Grissom, whose Mercury capsule sank in the Atlantic after the explosive bolts on the hatch fired by mistake, had insisted on a new design. The new hatch wouldn't release accidentally, but it took almost two minutes to open, which was a problem in an emergency.

The other mistake was the use of pure oxygen inside the capsule. The air we breathe is only 21 percent oxygen, and fire needs oxygen to burn. The higher the concentration of oxygen, the more dangerous a fire can be—things that would not normally burn can ignite. However, pure oxygen had been used in the Mercury and Gemini capsules with no problems. Engineers at North American recommended against using pure oxygen, but NASA decided it was fine.

As the February 21 launch date approached, problems mounted. The capsule's environmental controls malfunctioned, and coolant leaked from tubing. And wiring ran everywhere. There were *miles* of wiring inside the capsule, and it was easy to damage.

Gus Grissom knew there were problems with the spacecraft. In late January he picked a lemon off a tree in his backyard and hung it in the training simulator at the Cape. It was his not-so-subtle message to everyone: this capsule is a piece of junk.

Fire!

The test on January 27 was a "plugs out" test. It wasn't considered hazardous because the rocket was not filled with fuel. The astronauts would go through a simulated launch at Pad 34, and at some point the rocket would be disconnected from the tower. Would the power, life support, and communications systems work on their own?

Engineers had been having so many problems with the communications system that both Deke Slayton and manager Joe Shea had considered sitting in the capsule's lower equipment bay during the test, below the astronauts, so that at least they could hear what their problems were.

Early in the afternoon, Gus Grissom said he smelled something strange, like sour milk, in the oxygen pumped through his space suit. Unable to

The crew of Apollo 1 (l to r): Gus Grissom, Ed White, and Roger Chaffee. *Courtesy of NASA, S67-19770*

figure out the source, the test continued. More and more oxygen was pumped into the sealed capsule.

With the hatch closed, the crew continued to have trouble communicating with those outside. "How are we going to get to the moon if we can't even talk between three buildings?" Grissom snapped. At 6:20 PM the test was halted to work on the radio problems.

At 6:31 PM a spark from a frayed wire in the equipment bay below Grissom's feet caused the wire's insulation to start burning. The flames quickly spread to other wires in the bundle, then ignited the nylon netting below the three men.

Ed White shouted into his microphone. "Fire!"

The controller didn't know if he'd heard him correctly. (In fact, there has never been agreement on precisely what was said and by whom—the recording is difficult to understand.)

Then White called out, "We've got a fire in the cockpit!"

The burned Apollo 1 capsule, still in the White Room. *Courtesy of NASA, KSC-BurntCapsule*

The charred interior of the Apollo 1 capsule. *Courtesy of NASA, S67-21294*

A TV camera pointed at the hatch window showed White struggling to undo the hatch bolts, which required a tool.

"We have a bad fire," reported Chaffee. "We're burning up!" Everything that was flammable inside the capsule was now burning—foam pads, nylon tubing, even the Velcro stuck on the walls. In seconds, the temperature shot up to 2,500°F, and the pressure inside the capsule rose until its welds ruptured. Technicians rushed toward the capsule, only to be driven back by the heat, smoke, and flames.

The last thing controllers heard over the radio was a final, painful scream.

Back in Houston at Mission Control, the computer readouts went dead. Most assumed the worst. "I've never seen a facility or a group of people . . . so shaken in their entire lives," Gene Kranz recalled. "The majority of the controllers were kids fresh out of college in their early twenties. Everyone had gone through this agony of listening to this crew over the sixteen seconds. . . . It was very fresh, very real, and there were many

of the controllers who just couldn't seem to cope with this disaster that had occurred."

It would be five minutes before the technicians got the hatch open. When they did, pad leader Don Babbitt radioed, "I can't tell you what I see."

That Friday, Alan Bean was working at the Astronaut Office in Houston when a call came from Mike Collins. "We've lost the crew," Collins said. Bean was given the task of contacting the astronauts and other staff who would break the news to the families. The media were not notified until after the families were told.

Dark Days

After the autopsies, the bodies of Gus Grissom and Roger Chaffee were taken to Arlington National Cemetery for burial. On January 31, a bitterly cold day, the remaining six Mercury astronauts and John Young, Grissom's Gemini partner, accompanied his flag-draped casket to the grave. Four hours later, Chaffee was laid to rest beside Grissom as jets flew overhead in a "missing man formation." President Johnson was on hand along with the men's widows, parents, and children.

Later that day, Ed White was laid to rest at West Point, from which he had graduated in 1952. Six astronauts from his Gemini days—Armstrong, Aldrin, Conrad, Borman, Lovell, and Stafford— were honorary pallbearers.

The funerals were broadcast across the nation on live TV. Condolences came from around the world, including from the Soviet cosmonauts. "The death of these brave conquerors of space not only shocked the American people but caused deep pain in our hearts as well," they wrote.

The year also saw the first cosmonaut die. On his second flight into space, this time aboard Soyuz 1, Vladimir Komarov ran into trouble as soon as his spacecraft reached orbit and its solar panel wouldn't open. With its electrical power failing, the capsule's guidance computers and thrusters malfunctioned and it tumbled out of control. When the spacecraft finally reentered the atmosphere on April 24, its parachute tangled and it crashed to Earth.

NASA administrator James Webb sent a letter of condolence to Moscow. In it, he proposed that the two programs work together to make their spacecraft safer. "Could the lives already lost have been saved if we had known each other's hopes, aspirations, and plans?" he wrote. "Or could they have been saved if full cooperation had been the order of the day?"

Two more astronauts also died that year, though not in space. On June 6, Edward Givens was killed in an auto accident near the Manned Spaceflight Center in Houston, and on October 5, C. C. Williams perished after his T-38 had a mechanical failure and crashed near Tallahassee, Florida.

There would be no Apollo flights in 1967, and many worried about what the future held for the program. "I remember being at Arlington that day burying a couple of my colleagues back in '67," Gene Cernan remembered, "and I wasn't sure whether we were burying the entire Apollo program at that moment in time, or whether we were simply burying a couple of our friends."

But others recalled what Gus Grissom had said at a press conference in 1966: "If we die, we want people to accept it. We are in a risky business, and we hope that if anything happens to us, it will not delay the program. The conquest of space is worth the risk of life."

Lessons Learned

The day after the fire, NASA formed the Apollo 204 Review Board to investigate. (Apollo 204 was the original name of the mission, but it was later changed to Apollo 1.) Over the next nine weeks the board would tear apart the charred capsule piece by piece—not just to find the cause of the fire but also to identify any other problems that NASA and its contractors might have overlooked.

One of the first things the investigators learned was that the crew had not burned to death. Smoke and carbon monoxide from the fire had entered their suits and they asphyxiated—the men suffocated and passed out from lack of oxygen. Investigators also believed the wire that caused the blaze had been damaged when somebody either stepped on it or nicked it while the capsule was being built or modified.

But the most damning evidence came from other astronauts. They felt there was nobody at North American Aviation to whom they could talk about problems they saw, and NASA wasn't much better. Sloppy workmanship and sloppy oversight.

The board recommended that individual astronauts be given a stronger role in overseeing all aspects of the project and have more authority to call out problems they found. Work would have to be done correctly, even if it meant not reaching the moon before the end of the decade.

Nevertheless, they still *did* intend to meet Kennedy's challenge. The day after NASA issued its report, Deke Slayton called a meeting of 18 of its most experienced astronauts. When he arrived he got right to the point. "The guys who are going to fly the first lunar missions are right here in this room," he said, "and the first lunar landing crew is looking at me right now." But he didn't say who.

Among the 1,341 design changes made to the capsule and launchpad were to use nonflammable materials wherever possible, replace the hatch with one that that opened outward in three seconds, and install fire prevention systems at the launchpad. Guenter Wendt, who had run launchpad operations during Gemini, but not Apollo, was rehired as well. He was told to come up with an escape plan for the pad. Everyone had to get to safety in less than two minutes.

Despite the NASA review board's work, the US Congress opened its own investigation. Some at NASA believed they would use the hearings to shut down the Apollo program altogether. But then astronaut Frank Borman, who was on the review board, confronted the lawmakers. "We are confident in our management, our engineering, and ourselves," he said. "I think the question is, are *you* confident in *us*."

In the end, three people lost their jobs, but Apollo was allowed to continue. In a strange way, the fire might have even made the eventual moon landing possible. "We were given the gift

of time," astronaut Neil Armstrong recalled. "We didn't want that gift, but we were given months and months to not only fix the spacecraft, but rethink all our previous decisions, plans, and strategies, and change a lot of things, hopefully for the better."

"All-Up" with Apollo 4

While NASA worked on its problems with the command module, work progressed on the Saturn V. Three Saturn 1Bs (the smaller rocket) had been launched in 1966, before the fire. But now it was time for an "all-up" test of the Saturn V. Apollo 4 would be an unmanned flight. It was also a chance to test the enormous new Launch Complex 39, which had been built for Apollo.

On November 9, 1967, Apollo 4 was ready for launch. The rocket carried an unmanned command module and a dummy moon lander. Together they weighed 140 tons, more weight than NASA had sent into orbit on its previous 350 rocket flights *combined*. The Saturn V was that powerful.

But few realized how powerful. CBS news anchor Walter Cronkite broadcast a live report from a studio trailer parked more than three miles away. When the engines fired at 7:00 AM, a great sound blast rolled over the marshland.

"My God, our building's shaking here—our building's shaking!" Cronkite shouted as the studio's ceiling panels began to fall around him. "This big glass window is shaking! We're holding it with our hands! Look at that rocket GO! Into the clouds at 3,000 feet! The roar is terrific!" People as

far away as Jacksonville, 180 miles north, could see the bright fireball rise into the morning sky.

The Apollo 4 capsule made two circular orbits of the Earth before firing its stage-three engine to push it up into an elliptical orbit. The lopsided oval path took the capsule from 53 to 11,232 miles high. From there, it plummeted back to Earth. The capsule's rockets were fired to increase its speed to nearly 25,000 mph. Flights from the moon would return to Earth at this speed, and engineers needed to test the capsule's heat shield.

The spacecraft screamed into the atmosphere over the western Pacific Ocean. Its heat shield hit a temperature of 5,000°F, but the capsule's interior never rose above 70°F. Less than nine hours after it blasted off from Florida, Apollo 4 splashed down and was recovered by the USS *Bennington*.

More Missions—Apollo 5 and Apollo 6

Ten weeks after Apollo 4, the next test flight was ready. Apollo 5 would be the first in-space test of the lunar module (LM), the spacecraft that would eventually land on the moon. On January 22, 1968, it rode atop the Saturn 1B that Apollo 1 had been attached to during the fire.

During its 11 hours in orbit, the LM's descent and ascent engines were fired several times. In a moon landing, the descent engine would lower the LM to the surface. The ascent engine would be used to blast off the moon to return home. The controllers also simulated a landing abort, where the ascent engine was fired while the descent

Apollo 4 saw the first launch of the Saturn V, November 9, 1967.
Courtesy of NASA, S67-50433

engine was still attached. They called this a "fire in the hole" test. Though there were a few problems during the flight, NASA felt the Apollo 5 flight was a success.

Three months later the last unmanned mission, Apollo 6, was launched into space. Barely. As it rose through the atmosphere, the Saturn V shook up and down about five or six times a second. This "pogo bounce" caused fuel leaks, and two of the rocket's five stage-two engines shut down early. The bounces also knocked off two large panels that would have protected the LM during moon missions.

Frozen Rocket

If you've ever watched the liftoff of a liquid-fuel rocket like the Saturn V, you've seen white sheets of ice dropping off as the rocket clears the tower. Ice in Florida? What's happening?

The Saturn V used kerosene and liquid oxygen (LOX) to fuel its stage-one engines, and LOX and liquid hydrogen in stage two. LOX must be stored at -293°F or colder, and liquid hydrogen at -424°F. Both made the outside surface of the Saturn V very cold, causing water vapor from the humid Florida air to condense on the rocket, like a "sweaty" glass of iced tea on a humid day. And because the surface was so cold, the water would freeze in sheets of ice.

You can re-create a frozen rocket without leaving your home.

YOU'LL NEED

- Can of spray air (for cleaning electronics)
- Humid day

1. This demonstration works best on a humid day. Check your weather forecast—the dew point must be 65°F or higher. (If you live in a dry climate, run a hot shower in the bathroom with the door closed until it gets steamy.)

2. Shake up a can of spray air and place it on a table or counter, facing away from you. Squeeze the trigger and hold it open, trying not to touch the can, until it runs out of air. What happens to the outside of the can?

3. Touch the can—what do you feel? Now imagine this on a much, much larger scale.

Still, the command module made it into a wobbly orbit at 13,810 miles. But problems continued. Controllers tried to fire the third stage another time, and failed. Because of this, they were not able to test the command module's heat shield during reentry.

Chris Kraft was brutally honest about what had happened. "This was a disaster. I want to emphasize that. It was a disaster," he said. But the problems of the April 4 launch were largely ignored by the press for an understandable reason: Martin Luther King Jr. was assassinated the same day.

Apollo 7, Wally's Flight

Five weeks after the Apollo 1 fire, astronauts Wally Schirra, Walt Cunningham, and Donn Eisele were visiting Cape Kennedy when Deke Slayton paid them a surprise visit. "I want to let you guys know that you have the next flight," he said.

Wally Schirra was the perfect choice for commander. He had been to space twice before. People who worked at NASA adored "Jolly Wally." So did the American public.

After the crew was announced they became a key part of the effort to rebuild confidence in the program. When not training, the astronauts were paraded around the country to speak to civic groups and Apollo contractors. The message was clear: *We are not going to let this setback keep us from reaching the moon.*

"Apollo 7 became very important. If we had not had a success on Apollo 7, we really don't know what would've happened to the space program,"

Walt Cunningham admitted. "Another accident and the fainthearted in the country . . . would've been clamoring to stop it."

Behind the scenes, however, Schirra was not the same happy-go-lucky guy. "As the months went by and we began getting closer to launch, Wally Schirra started to change," observed Guenter Wendt. "The 'Jolly Wally' we had always known was replaced by a man with high expectations and a relatively short fuse." Schirra resisted changes to the flight plan if he felt they weren't critical to the mission—scientific experiments, television broadcasts, and photography.

When Schirra learned the couches that the astronauts were strapped to during launch and splashdown had not been updated, he demanded that Mission Control adopt a new rule: if the wind speed at the launchpad was greater than 18 knots (about 21 mph), the flight would be scrubbed. He was concerned that, in an emergency abort, the parachutes on the escape tower could blow the capsule back onto land and the astronauts could be injured.

On September 20, three weeks before the launch, Schirra announced that he would be retiring from NASA the following July. Apollo 7 would be his final spaceflight.

Back in Business

On October 11, 1968, Apollo 7 was ready. NASA staff lined the hallway and applauded as the three astronauts marched out to a van that would carry them to Pad 34. This was the same launchpad

SURFING THROUGH EARTH'S ATMOSPHERE

When the Apollo command module returned to Earth, it didn't drop like a stone into the ocean. Instead, it took an up-and-down path, like a surfer riding a wave. Sometimes it turned its flat heat shield at an angle to slide through the atmosphere, causing the capsule to rise before plunging again. Once it reached its target, it would release its parachutes and drop straight down.

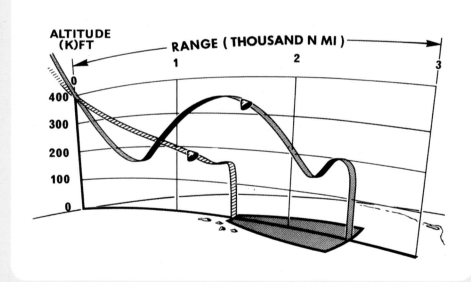

The Apollo command module could take different paths to reach its target. *From* Apollo Logistics Training Manual *(North American Aviation, 1965), author's collection*

STAR TREK

In the early years of the Apollo program, from 1966 to 1969, *Star Trek* debuted on television. Each episode opened with Captain Kirk proclaiming, "Space: the final frontier. These are the voyages of the starship *Enterprise*. Its five-year mission: to explore strange new worlds, to seek out new life and new civilizations,

The original cast of *Star Trek* and its creator, Gene Roddenberry, at the rollout of the Space Shuttle *Enterprise*, 1976. *Courtesy of NASA, S91-27436*

to boldly go where no man has gone before." The opening reminded many of President Kennedy's challenge.

Not surprisingly, many astronauts and NASA personnel were big fans of the show. One episode in the second season, "Assignment: Earth," had Captain Kirk and Mr. Spock traveling back in time to a Saturn V launch, which used actual footage from early Apollo flights. The series' final episode aired just a month before the Apollo 11 landing.

In the 1970s, NASA hired Nichelle Nichols, who played communications officer Lieutenant Uhura, to help it recruit women and people of color to apply to its astronaut program. Both Sally Ride, the first US woman in space (June 1983), and Guion Bluford, the first African American in space (August 1983), were recruited with her help. And when the Space Shuttle program began, its first working vehicle—which never went to space—was named the *Enterprise*.

where the Apollo 1 crew had died 21 months earlier, and was the last time it would be used.

At the tower, Guenter Wendt and his crew loaded the astronauts into the capsule and closed the hatch. The countdown continued as Launch Control monitored the rocket and weather. At one point, Schirra looked out the window and remarked, "It's as blue as a bluebird out there."

The sky may have been clear, but the weather was not cooperating. "It was quite windy,"

Cunningham recalled. "Beneath us we could feel the vehicle and the swing-arm sway." Schirra reminded Launch Control of his wind speed rule.

Back in Houston, Jo Schirra watched the television broadcast with her children and most of the other Mercury Seven's families. At her home, Harriet Eisele had three TVs on—one for each network—and tightly held her four-year-old son Jon on her lap. She also wore a *Peanuts* button on her sweater that read, I've Developed a New

PHILOSOPHY. I ONLY DREAD ONE DAY AT A TIME. Lo Cunningham, Walt's wife, had brought their two children to Florida to view the launch from a boat on the nearby Banana River.

As the 10:00 AM liftoff approached, gusts at the tower were 20 to 25 knots, just above what Schirra considered dangerous. But CapCom Tom Stafford assured him that everything was fine. (The CapCom was the "capsule communicator," the person chosen to communicate between Houston and the crew during a mission. The CapCom was usually an astronaut.) Schirra wasn't happy, but he trusted Stafford, who had flown with him on Gemini 6.

The seconds ticked down and Cunningham mumbled to himself, "OK, Cunningham, whatever you do, *don't screw up.*" The engines fired, the Saturn 1B slowly lifted off the pad, and 12 seconds later it cleared the tower. Soon Apollo 7 was orbiting the Earth at 17,500 mph.

Live from the Apollo Room

"You don't really know what togetherness is until you have spent 11 days with two other people in a volume about the size of a back seat in a large American sedan," Walt Cunningham wrote of Apollo 7. "If your buddy belched, you said 'Excuse me.' We worked, ate, slept, caught colds, and performed all bodily functions in that same space."

He wasn't kidding. On the day of the launch, Schirra felt he was coming down with something. A day later, in orbit, he had a full-blown head cold. Then Eisele caught it. And as they soon learned,

snot doesn't drain in zero gravity. Schirra was constantly blowing his nose. "Within a short time we were stuffing used tissues in every unused spot we could find," Cunningham wrote.

Nevertheless, the crew had work to do. Their flight was designed to test the command and service module (CSM) and its navigation system, and how three astronauts could work together during the time it would take to travel to the moon and back.

On the second day, the crew maneuvered the capsule to within 70 feet of Saturn's second-stage booster. By that time, the booster was tumbling out of control and the astronauts didn't want to fly too close to it. Schirra was so focused on the test he became angry when Mission Control reminded him about the upcoming television broadcast. He felt it was a waste of the crew's time. "We have a new vehicle up here, and I can tell you [at] this point TV will be delayed without any further discussion," he barked. The first live broadcast from space was pushed from Saturday to Sunday.

On the following evening, a fuzzy black-and-white picture appeared on television screens across the globe. Wally Schirra held up a printed sign: FROM THE LOVELY APOLLO ROOM HIGH ATOP EVERYTHING. Viewers enjoyed shots of Earth and watched the astronauts perform acrobatics in zero gravity—Cunningham had been a college gymnast. Astronauts gave a tour of the command module and showed how food was prepared in space. Schirra also held up another sign: KEEP THOSE CARDS AND LETTERS COMING IN FOLKS. A few days later his secretary was swamped with 3,000 letters,

Courtesy of NASA, 68-26668

Donn Eisele (left) and Wally Schirra during the first live TV broadcast from space, October 14, 1968. *Courtesy of NASA, S68-50713*

and she asked Mission Control to tell him never to do that again.

There were seven live shows during the mission. Each was seven to eleven minutes long, broadcast when the capsule passed over Texas or Kennedy Space Center, which had the only radar dishes that could pick up a TV signal.

Short Tempers

The astronauts may have looked happy during the broadcasts, but Wally Schirra continued to make the crew's life difficult. Mission Control wasn't any happier. Every time they made a change to the flight plan, Schirra would complain.

Finally, he snapped. "I have had it up here today," Schirra said. "And from now on, I'm going to be an onboard flight director for these updates. We are not going to accept any new games . . .

or doing some crazy tests we never heard of before." In truth, Schirra hadn't paid much attention to the science experiments during training, so the requests often seemed new, even when they weren't.

As the days rolled on, there was less and less to do. "The last several days were fairly boring," Cunningham confessed. "We were out of film. . . . We'd accomplished all these things. We could've done a lot of other activities."

"I spent a good part of the day passes looking out the windows at the silent, awesome spectacle of the earth sailing majestically by," said Eisele.

Because of the Apollo 1 fire, the crew was not allowed to bring along books, cards, or anything paper. To pass the time, they invented zero-gravity space games. "Walt Cunningham would make a ring with his thumb and forefinger, and I would try to shoot a pen through the ring," said Schirra. During meals they would fling cinnamon cubes at each other and try to catch them in their mouths, or deflect them with blasts from an air gun. But even that kept them entertained only so long. "I was *bored to tears*," Schirra admitted.

Return to Earth

After nearly 11 days in orbit, it was time to return. Yet there was still time for one last argument with Mission Control. Schirra knew that the pressure inside the capsule would change as they returned to Earth. The crew's sinuses were still stuffed up, and Schirra worried they wouldn't be able to clear their ears if they wore their helmets. How could

How Big Was the Command Module?

The Apollo command module was a tight fit for three astronauts. Its inside height was a little more than 9 feet, the same as most home ceilings, but cone shaped. In this activity, you will use yarn to re-create the shape of the command module to get an idea of how big it really was . . . or wasn't.

YOU'LL NEED

- Large room
- Yarn
- Tape measure
- Painter's tape
- Stepladder
- 8 heavy books
- Adult helper
- 2 friends

1. Using a tape measure, cut eight 12-foot lengths of yarn.

2. Hold one end of each piece together and tie them into a knot.

3. Ask an adult to use a stepladder and painter's tape (to prevent damage) to stick the knot to the ceiling in the center of a large room. Move furniture if necessary.

4. Measure out 6½ feet from where the yarn hangs to the floor. Gently pull one strand of yarn out to that point and hold it in place with a heavy book. The string should not sag.

5. Measure 6½ feet in the opposite direction, then hold a second length of yarn in place with another book.

6. Repeat this process with the remaining yarn and books. It should look like a cone when done.

7. Stand inside the "capsule" with two of your friends. Can you imagine flying to the moon in a spacecraft this size, for a week or more?

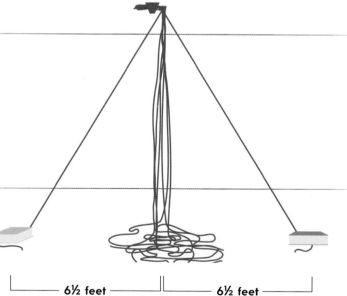

├──── 6½ feet ────┤├──── 6½ feet ────┤

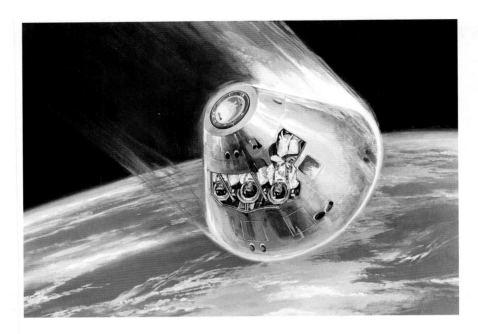

you "pop" your ears if you couldn't hold or blow your nose? Would the pressure rupture their eardrums? So, even though it went against the rules, Schirra said they would not wear their helmets during reentry.

Mission Control was angry. Deke Slayton came on the radio. "Please Wally, put the helmets on."

"Sorry, Deke," Schirra replied. "Unless you can come up here and put them on for us, we're coming home with the helmets off."

Apollo 7 splashed down in the Atlantic near Bermuda. For the first few minutes, the capsule was upside down, bobbing in the waves as the astronauts hung from their seat harnesses.

"How do you feel?" Eisele asked the others. "You going to get sick? I think I'm going to throw up." He was right—he barfed before the "uprighting bags" inflated to turn the capsule back over.

The crew were lifted onto a helicopter and flown to the nearby USS *Essex* aircraft carrier. They were still getting used to the feeling of gravity when they landed on the deck. Cunningham remembered that "even our clothes seemed heavy. When we stepped out of the helicopter onto the carrier, we all had the uneasy feeling that our pants were going to fall off. I hitched mine up and the three of us grinned crazily as we realized why."

Despite the disagreements between the ground and crew, Apollo 7 was a successful mission. General Sam Phillips, director of the Apollo program, called it "101% successful" because it achieved every goal they set, plus some. But the crew's behavior still angered many in Mission Control. Chris Kraft was said to have grumbled, "These guys'll never fly again." And none did.

Eat Like an Astronaut

NASA tested new and improved types of "space food" on Apollo 7. Gemini astronauts had complained about their meals. Now they were given 70 options, including strawberry cereal bites, pea soup, hot dogs, chicken and vegetables, banana pudding, and cheese cracker cubes. Dietitians would come up with balanced meals from the crew's favorites. Astronauts were also given edible toothpaste.

Many of the foods were dehydrated. The crew had to inject hot or cold water into the plastic meal bags before eating. Follow this "recipe" to see what it is like to eat like an astronaut—no plates or utensils!

YOU'LL NEED

- Small box of instant pudding mix
- Milk
- 2 resealable plastic bags
- Scissors

1. Divide a small box of instant pudding mix between two resealable plastic bags.

2. Add milk to the mix according to the directions on the box, putting half in each bag.

3. Zip each bag until *almost* closed and squeeze out as much air as possible. Then seal it closed.

4. Carefully squish the bag to combine the mix with the milk. Refrigerate according to the directions.

5. Once ready, eat . . . but without utensils. Use scissors to cut off one corner of the bag, then squeeze the pudding into your mouth. Can you imagine the problems you'd have doing this in zero gravity?

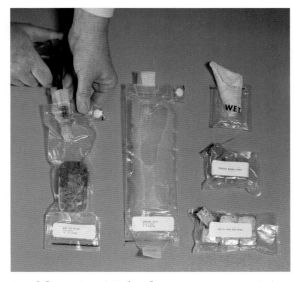

Food from Gemini: beef pot roast, orange juice, a wet napkin, toasted bread cubes, and bacon-and-egg bites. Notice the valves to inject water into the roast beef and orange juice. *Courtesy of NASA, S65-10971*

4

To the Moon and Back

Apollo 8 launched on December 21, 1968. For the first two hours it orbited the Earth while the crew—Frank Borman, Jim Lovell, and Bill Anders—and Mission Control made sure everything was working fine. It was.

Finally, CapCom Mike Collins radioed, "Alright, Apollo 8. You are Go for TLI."

Jeez, there's got to be a better way of saying this, thought Collins. For the first time in history, humans were leaving the gravitational bonds of Earth. TLI stood for "translunar injection," a technical way of saying, "Head off to the moon." Perhaps, Collins thought, he should "invoke Christopher Columbus or a primordial reptile coming up out of the swamps onto dry land for the first time, or . . . go back through the sweep of history and say something very, very meaningful." But he didn't get the chance.

The Apollo 8 crew, (front to back) Frank Borman, Jim Lovell, and Bill Anders, head off to the launchpad, December 21, 1968.
Courtesy of NASA, S68-55999

Borman broke in: "Roger. We understand we are Go for TLI."

When Jim Lovell punched the TLI command into the guidance computer, the display lit up: 99. It was the computer's way of asking, "Are you sure?" Lovell then pushed the button marked PROCEED.

Shoot for the Moon

In the summer of 1968 a CIA spy satellite photographed something ominous at the Soviet Union's space launch facility: a powerful new rocket that could launch a larger capsule than ever before. It was called Zond, and even though it was not capable of *landing on* the moon, it could possibly fly *around* the moon with a crew of two . . . before the Americans. Worse still, Apollo was behind schedule. The first lunar module (LM) wouldn't be ready until early 1969. NASA wanted to fly the LM in Earth orbit before sending it to the moon. Then in September 1968 the Russians sent Zond 5 around the moon and back. The capsule carried two live turtles, mealworms, wine flies, plants, seeds, and a human mannequin.

But NASA had its own secrets. Administrator George Low had come up with a bold plan: a trip to the moon *without* the LM. And not just to fly by the moon—the Apollo crew would orbit the moon once it got there, not swing around it and fly directly back.

"Are you out of your mind?!" shouted NASA director James Webb when told about Low's idea. Apollo hadn't even launched a Saturn V with a crew. "If these three men are stranded out there and die in lunar orbit, no one—lovers, poets, no one—will ever look at the moon the same way again," Webb said.

The astronauts were far less concerned. Deke Slayton broke the news to Frank Borman. "We want to change Apollo 8 from an Earth orbital to a lunar orbital flight," he said. "I know that doesn't give us much time, so I have to ask you: Do you want to do it or not?"

Borman didn't hesitate. "Yes." Slayton claimed the usually calm Borman "almost turned handsprings." He didn't even ask the rest of his crew, but they soon agreed.

"I was elated! I thought, *Man, this is great!*" recalled Jim Lovell. "I didn't want to spend another eleven days . . . going around the earth again." And "the fact that we were going to plow new ground, that we were going to explore unknown areas, that we were going to see the far side of the moon for the first time—this aspect of going to the moon was so great that any risks that were involved were miniscule, in *my* estimation."

Bill Anders was more concerned for his family than he was for himself. He and his wife, Valerie, had five young children. What would happen to them if he didn't return? But when Bill told Valerie, she asked, "Isn't this what you want to do?" Bill said yes, it was.

Jim Lovell broke the news to his wife, Marilyn, when she mentioned the family's upcoming trip to Mexico. "I can't go on vacation," he said.

Marilyn wasn't happy. "I've already made all these plans for Acapulco!" she said.

"I'm going somewhere else," he said. "Someplace special."

"Where are you going?" she asked.

"Would you believe, the moon?" Jim replied, smiling.

Preparing to Leave

On November 12, 1968, two weeks after Apollo 7, NASA's Thomas Paine announced, "After a careful and thorough examination of all the systems and risks involved, we have concluded that we are now ready to fly the most advanced mission for Apollo 8 launched in December—the orbit around the moon."

It shouldn't have come as a surprise. Two days before Apollo 7 launched from Pad 34, NASA rolled out a Saturn V to Pad 39. Everybody could see it, and the Saturn V was used for just one thing: leaving Earth orbit.

To break free of Earth's gravitational pull, Apollo 8 would have to accelerate to more than 25,000 mph—"escape velocity"—from its orbiting speed of 17,500 mph. The moon orbits the Earth at 2,288 mph, so the capsule would have to aim for the point in space where the moon would be three days after launch.

The moon is 240,000 miles from Earth, so why would it take three days to get there if Apollo 8 was moving at 25,000 mph? Wouldn't it take just 10 hours? In reality, a spacecraft is more like a roller coaster than an airplane. Once Apollo 8 reached escape velocity, it would coast the rest of the way to the moon. The Earth's gravity would continue

Design a Mission Patch

Every NASA mission had its own insignia, which the astronauts wore as a patch. Jim Lovell designed the Apollo 8 insignia. It was cone shaped, like the command module, and showed the flight's path to the moon and back, which formed the shape of the number eight.

In this activity, imagine you've been selected for the first trip to Mars. Design a patch for your historic journey.

YOU'LL NEED

- Paper
- Colored pencils or markers

Courtesy of NASA, S68-51093

1. Start by looking at the Apollo insignias in this book. What design elements were used in each patch? All had the mission's name, but not every insignia had the astronauts' names, or showed an image of the spacecraft.

2. Make a list of the elements you want to include.

3. Draw a few sketches to help you decide on your final design.

4. Create a full-color version using colored pencils or markers.

PHASES OF AN APOLLO MISSION

Every Apollo mission to the moon went through the same basic phases. After **launch**, the spacecraft would "park" in **Earth orbit**. If there were no problems, the astronauts fired the third-stage engine for **translunar injection**, meaning they would be injected onto a path to the moon. Once on their way, the command and service module (CSM) would separate from the third stage, turn around, and dock with the lunar module (LM). This was called **transposition and docking**. The CSM would pull the LM away from the third stage and the joined spacecraft would coast to the moon—the **translunar coast**.

After the astronauts arrived at the moon, they would slow down the spacecraft using the CSM's engine in a maneuver called **lunar orbit insertion**. Once in orbit, the CSM and LM would separate. The LM would **land on the moon** with two astronauts, while the third remained in orbit in the CSM.

To return to Earth, the LM would launch from the moon's surface for a **lunar orbit rendezvous** with the CSM. It would do this by breaking in half, leaving behind its descent stage—the bottom half with the landing pads—and riding in the ascent stage—the top

Adapted from Apollo Logistics Training Manual *(North American Aviation, 1965), author's collection*

half. After joining the CSM, the LM's ascent stage would be detached (and often deliberately crashed into the moon). The astronauts would then fire the CSM's engine for **transearth injection**. Like earlier, it would coast all the way home—the **transearth coast**. Just before reaching Earth, the **CSM would separate** into two pieces: the command module (CM), which held the astronauts, and the service module (SM), where the engine was located. The CM would burn back through the atmosphere and splash down in the ocean—the **entry and landing**. Easy!

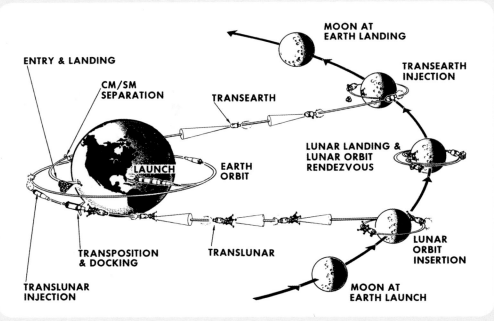

to pull on it, slowing it down bit by bit. Like a roller coaster heading uphill, it moves fastest at the bottom, but slows until it reaches the top.

So many things could go wrong on this mission. The engine could fail to reach escape velocity. The capsule could head in the wrong direction and miss the moon entirely. The spacecraft could fail to enter lunar orbit and crash to the surface or shoot off into deep space.

The astronauts' families were worried. "As much as I tried to hide my fears, even from myself, it was not easy on any of us, and it wasn't easy on our children," recalled Marilyn Lovell.

Susan Borman tried to put on a brave face for the press. "We'd say how proud we were, how confident we were, and then I'd go back in the house and kick a door in," she admitted.

Borman no doubt recalled a conversation she'd had with Chris Kraft after learning about the mission. "Hey Chris. I'd really appreciate it if you would level with me. I really, really, want to know what you think their chances are of getting home," she said.

"OK, how's fifty-fifty?" he said.

Saying Goodbye

Two days before launch, Jim and Marilyn Lovell stood on the beach, gazing at the Saturn V, which was bathed in spotlights against the night sky. Jim pulled out a photo of the moon's surface and pointed to a triangular mountain near the Sea of Tranquility.

"I'm going to name that mountain for you," he said. Mount Marilyn. Years earlier she had typed his college term paper about rocket travel, and now it was happening. Two days later she would watch the launch with their four children from a nearby sand dune and think about how happy her husband must be to achieve his lifelong dream.

The day before launch, a few visitors surprised the crew for lunch—66-year-old aviator Charles Lindbergh, his wife, Anne Morrow Lindbergh,

The Apollo 8 crew with the CM simulator (l to r): Jim Lovell, Bill Anders, and Frank Borman. *Courtesy of NASA, S68-50265*

How Far Away Is the Moon?

It's hard to get an idea of the sizes and distances involved in spaceflight. But you can make a simple model of the Earth and moon using sports equipment.

YOU'LL NEED

🌙 Basketball

🌙 Tennis ball

🌙 Tape measure

🌙 String (optional)

123RF.com, © Aaron Amat

123RF.com, © Sergii Telesh

1. Hold a basketball and a tennis ball side by side. If the Earth were the size of a basketball, the moon would be about the size of the tennis ball. Compared to the "Earth," is the "moon" as big as you thought it would be? Smaller?

2. Now calculate how far apart the balls should be placed to make your model of the Earth and moon accurate. The moon is approximately 10 times as far from Earth as the circumference of the Earth—the distance around it at the equator. Measure the circumference of the basketball "Earth" in inches. If the tape measure won't curve around the ball, wrap a string around it, mark the length, and measure the string with a ruler.

3. Multiply that length by 10 for the distance between the "Earth" and "moon" in inches (answer below).

4. Place the basketball "Earth" on the ground and use a tape measure to determine how far away to place the tennis ball "moon." Are you surprised?

Answer: Basketball circumference = 30 inches; Distance between balls = 300 inches, or 25 feet and Wernher von Braun. Lindbergh told the astronauts that Robert Goddard had once calculated that a trip to the moon might cost $1 million, and everyone laughed. "We talked and talked and talked, and they stayed and stayed and stayed," Borman remembered.

That evening, back in Houston, neighbors stopped by the Anders home to sing Christmas carols and "The Star-Spangled Banner" for Valerie and the children. The entire family had celebrated the holiday earlier in the month. Quietly, Bill gave Valerie two cassette tapes, one to play on Christmas Day, and another to play if he didn't return.

Susan Borman had also stayed in Houston for the launch. She didn't sleep much the night before. Down at Cape Kennedy, Frank Borman couldn't sleep, either, and spent most of the night lying in his metal bed in the astronaut quarters, staring at the ceiling.

The crew was taken to Pad 39 early the next morning for a 7:51 AM launch. Anne Morrow Lindbergh wrote about it in *Life* magazine:

People stop talking, stand in front of their cars and raise binoculars to their eyes. We peer nervously at the launch site and then at our wristwatches. Radio voices blare unnaturally loud from car windows. "Now only 30 minutes to launch time. . . . 15 minutes. . . . 6 minutes. . . . 30 seconds to go. . . . 20. . . . T minus 15, 14, 13, 12, 11, 10, 9. . . . *Ignition!*" . . . "Ahhhh." The crowd gasps, almost in unison. . . . Suddenly the noise breaks, jumps across our three separating miles—a shattering roar of explosions, a trip-hammer over one's head, under one's feet, through one's body. The earth shakes; cars rattle; vibrations beat in the chest. A roll of thunder, prolonged, prolonged, prolonged. . . . The foreground is now full of birds; a great flock of ducks, herons, small birds rises pell-mell from the marshes at the noise. Fluttering in alarm and confusion, they scatter in all directions as if it were the end of the world.

"As we lifted off . . . we were literally being thrown around," Bill Anders remembered. "I felt like a rat in the jaws of a giant terrier." Eleven and a half minutes later, Apollo 8 was in Earth orbit. Frank Borman turned to Anders, the rookie, and warned him, "I don't want to see you looking out the window!" There was a lot to do before they left orbit.

Over in the Soviet Union, Lev Kamanin, a Kremlin space official, wrote in his diary, "For us this [day] is darkened with the realization of lost opportunities and with sadness that today the men flying to the moon are named Borman, Lovell, and Anders, and not Bykovsky, Popovich, and Leonov."

Coasting Uphill

Two and a half hours after Apollo 8 entered Earth orbit, Mission Control gave the OK to fire the stage-three engine. Twelve minutes later, right on schedule, Lovell punched the button to proceed.

Forearm at 7 Gs

During liftoff, astronauts felt a force from the rocket's acceleration. It's the same thing you feel on some amusement park rides, only stronger. Their bodies could feel seven times heavier than they did on Earth. Even lifting an arm to push a button could be difficult, especially with the capsule violently shaking.

Just how heavy would your forearm feel at 7 Gs? (One G is the force you feel here on Earth.) This activity will show you.

YOU'LL NEED

- Bathroom scale
- Calculator
- Heavy objects
- Pillowcase

1. Measure your weight on a bathroom scale.
2. Calculate the weight of your forearm and hand, from elbow to fingertips. For most humans, it is 2.1 percent of one's body weight. Multiply your weight by 0.021 and write it down.
3. Multiply this number by 7 to determine your forearm's 7 G weight. Write it down.
4. Stack heavy objects, like books, on the bathroom scale until it measures the 7 G weight you calculated.
5. Place the objects in a pillowcase.
6. Lift the pillowcase. Can you imagine your forearm weighing this much? Try moving your arm around while holding this weight.

Bonus: Calculate your total weight during liftoff—multiply your measurement in step 1 by 7. Can you imagine what it would feel like?

The spacecraft started to rumble and the men were pushed back against their couches as it accelerated. Their eyes were trained on the control panels in front of them. Everything looked fine. The engine burned for exactly 318 seconds.

"You could've heard a pin drop in that control center," said Gerry Griffin. "And when the burn was performed—and it cut off right on the money—we all kind of just looked at one another. Without uttering a word, we all said the same thing: 'We just did it. We're headed to the moon.'"

The final step after TLI was to separate from the S-IVB engine. The crew fired explosive bolts to detach it from the CSM, then used the CSM's thrusters to move away from the now-useless third stage. The jolt surprised them all.

Now detached, the crew rotated the CSM so that its windows pointed back at Earth. They were shocked: the planet was visibly shrinking as they raced away. "You had to pinch yourself," Lovell recalled. "Hey, we're really going to the moon!"

On the mission's first day, Frank Borman vomited in the equipment bay. Lovell watched a chunky blob the size of a tennis ball float up from below and break in half. One half of the blob headed toward Lovell, who backed into a corner before it hit his jumpsuit and splattered like an egg.

NASA doctors feared Borman had caught the Hong Kong flu, which was spreading across the United States, or was suffering from radiation sickness. "I think we all started wondering, 'Maybe there's something about going to the moon that we don't understand,'" Gerry Griffin later admitted.

But neither Lovell nor Anders became ill, so doctors concluded it was motion sickness.

Borman recovered enough the next day that he could narrate a live TV broadcast. After trying and failing to film the Earth out the window, Anders turned the camera toward Lovell.

"Jim, what are you doing here?" Borman asked as Lovell injected water into a plastic bag filled with powder. "Jim is fixing dessert. He is making up a bag of chocolate pudding. You can see it come floating by." Lovell twirled the bag in zero gravity.

"This transmission is coming to you approximately halfway between the moon and the Earth," Borman went on. "We have been 31 hours and about 20 minutes into flight. We have about less than 40 hours left to go to the moon. You can see Bill's got his toothbrush here. He has been brushing his teeth regularly."

At the show's end, Lovell smiled at the camera. "Happy birthday, mother," he said. Blanch Lovell, who had encouraged her son's love of rockets, was celebrating her 73rd birthday.

"I just can't get over it," Blanch told a reporter. "When they had so many things to do in space that he would think of his mother on her birthday."

Lunar Orbit

Two days and eight hours into the flight, Apollo 8 reached the top of the hill—202,700 miles from Earth. At this point in space, known as the "equigravisphere," the pull of gravity from the Earth and the moon are the same. The spacecraft, which had slowed to 2,200 mph, would now begin

An artist's rendering of the Apollo 8 CSM separating from the Saturn V's third stage. *Courtesy of NASA, S68-51306*

accelerating toward the moon. Over the next 12 hours it gained speed, falling faster and faster.

"As a matter of interest, we have as yet to see the moon," Lovell reported. All this time the capsule had been flying backward, its engine pointed at the moon.

"Roger," the CapCom responded, "Apollo 8 . . . what else are you seeing?"

"Nothing," said Anders. "It's like being on the inside of a submarine."

Soon they would swing around the moon's far side, fire the SPS engine to slow down, and slip into orbit. All this would happen when the moon blocked any radio contact with Earth.

Moments before the radio cut off, CapCom Jerry Carr radioed, "Safe journey, guys."

THE COMMAND AND SERVICE MODULE

The Apollo **command and service module (CSM)** was a two-part spacecraft. The cone-shaped **command module (CM)** carried the astronauts from launch through splashdown. The cylindrical **service module (SM)** was attached behind it, and held the rocket fuel, batteries, fuel cells, water, and liquid oxygen and hydrogen tanks—most of what the CM needed to run. These essentials transferred through a **bus** on the side of the CSM.

The CM was 10½ feet tall and 13 feet in diameter. It had five **windows**—two at the side, two facing forward, and one in the **main hatch**. The crew rode on "couches" that were more like cots, cloth slung over metal frames. Beneath the couches, a lower equipment bay held space suits, food, cameras, medical kits, and other material the crew needed.

At the top, nose end of the CM was a short tunnel and **docking hatch** that connected to the lunar module (see page 68). At the base of the CM was the heat shield.

The service module was 13 feet long, 23 feet counting the main rear engine, the **service propulsion system (SPS)** engine. The SPS engine could generate 20,500 pounds of thrust, and was used to maneuver the CSM into and out of lunar orbit.

Around the outside of the CSM were four **reaction control engines**, each with four thrusters that could turn the CSM and keep it on course. A large **high-gain (deep space) antenna** at the rear of the CSM transmitted information back to Earth. During flight, the CSM rotated in passive thermal control mode—everyone called it "barbeque mode"—to keep one side from getting too hot (250°F, from the sun) or too cold (-200°F, from deep space).

The CM and SM remained attached until 15 minutes before the capsule reentered the Earth's atmosphere. The SM burned up on reentry. The CM had six more reaction control engines to guide the capsule through the atmosphere. At five miles high, two drogue parachutes from the nose of the CM would slow down the spacecraft. Then, after it had slowed, three large main parachutes would open to drop the capsule the final two miles down to the ocean.

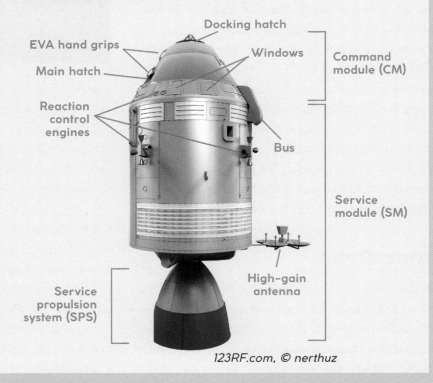

123RF.com, © nerthuz

"Thanks a lot, troops," replied Anders. Lovell added, "We'll see you on the other side."

"Apollo 8, ten seconds to go," reported Carr. "You're Go all the way."

"Roger," said Borman, and the radio went dead. He then turned to the others. "So? Are we Go for this thing?"

Apollo 8 then passed into the shadow of the moon. Without the sun's glare, millions of stars suddenly appeared. "God, there were stars . . . even the dimmest stars popped out," Anders remembered. "And yet there was this very sharp line. Absolutely no stars. *Total* blackness. And *that* was the moon. . . . I remember feeling this kind of *eeewww* feeling, just like somebody would suddenly have if you go running through a tunnel blindfolded."

Back in Houston, Valerie Anders waited. "These things seemed to happen at night. Always the middle of the night," she recalled. "Wives had brought food over and we had tea and coffee, and we were sitting around with the squawk box, waiting for this thing to occur." (Before each flight, NASA put a "squawk box" in each family's home, which would broadcast the live discussion between the astronauts and Mission Control.)

The minutes crept by. If the SPS engine didn't fire, the spacecraft would roar around the moon and be flung back toward Earth. If it fired for longer than 247 seconds, they would slow too much, and eventually crash to the surface. And if the engine fired for less than 247 seconds, the capsule would be flung out into space, never to return.

Thirty-four minutes after the last message, Carr began calling the spacecraft.

An artist's rendering of Apollo 8 firing the SPS engine on the far side of the moon. *Courtesy of NASA, S68-51302*

"Apollo 8, Houston. Over."

Nothing.

Carr repeated the call every 20 to 30 seconds— five times without an answer.

Finally, something. "Go ahead, Houston," Lovell said. "This is Apollo 8. Burn complete." Apollo 8 was in orbit around the moon.

Christmas Message

Apollo 8 reached the moon on Christmas Eve. The plan was to make 10 orbits over the next 20 hours. Jim Lovell admitted it was easy to be distracted.

EARTHRISE

On Christmas Eve, Apollo 8 was on its fourth orbit of the moon when the astronauts witnessed something no human had ever seen.

"Oh my God! Look at that picture over there!" Frank Borman shouted. "Here's the Earth coming up. Wow, is that pretty!"

"Hand me that roll of color [film], quick," Bill Anders said to Jim Lovell.

Earthrise. Not a sunrise or a moonrise, but our home planet emerging from the moon's horizon. Though not on the flight plan—mission planners didn't consider a photo of Earth from the moon very important—Anders snapped away. It wasn't until after the astronauts returned and NASA developed the film that anyone realized what they'd captured. "To me [it] looked like a Christmas tree ornament, coming up over this very stark, ugly lunar landscape," Anders recalled. "We came all this way to explore the moon, and the most important thing is that we discovered the earth."

Photographer Galen Rowell called *Earthrise* "the most influential environmental photograph ever taken." It appeared on magazine and newspaper covers in the weeks to follow, and was later placed on the first Earth Day flag, on April 22, 1970. Later that same year, Congress created the Environmental Protection Agency. Lovell recalled, "It made us realize we had a home with limited resources, and its inhabitants must learn to live and work together."

Courtesy of NASA, 68-HC-870

"We were like three school kids looking into a candy store window," he said. "I think we forgot the flight plan, we had our noses pressed against the glass, we were looking at those craters going by."

But this wasn't a sightseeing vacation—there was work to do. Most important, they needed to photograph the Sea of Tranquility, where NASA hoped to make the first landing.

The crew completed most of its tasks by the seventh orbit, so Borman ordered Lovell and Anders to get some rest. He would stay awake, monitoring the ship.

Later, at 9:30 PM in Houston, on their ninth orbit, the crew made a 24-minute television broadcast. About a billion viewers—one in four humans—watched.

"This is Apollo 8, coming to you live from the moon," Borman began, then explained what they had been up to during the previous 16 hours. And then Borman grew philosophical. "The moon is a different thing to each one of us. . . . I know my own impression is that it's a vast, lonely, forbidding-type existence, or expanse of nothing, that looks rather like clouds and clouds of pumice stone, and it certainly would not appear to be a very inviting place to live or work." He then asked Lovell, "Jim, what have you thought most about?"

"Well, Frank, my thoughts are very similar," said Lovell. "The vast loneliness up here of the moon is awe inspiring, and it makes you realize just what you have back there on Earth. The Earth from here is a grand oasis in the big vastness of space."

"Bill, what do you think?" Borman prodded.

"I think the thing that impressed me the most was the lunar sunrises and sunsets," replied Anders. "These in particular bring out the stark nature of the terrain."

Television viewers watched the lunar surface drift past the capsule window as the men pointed out craters and mountains and the Sea of Tranquility.

As they neared the end of the show, Bill Anders said, "We are now approaching the lunar sunrise, and for all the people back on Earth, the crew of Apollo 8 has a message that we would like to send to you."

It was a reading from Genesis. "In the beginning, God created the Heaven and the Earth. And the Earth was without form and void, and darkness was upon the face of the deep. And the spirit of God moved upon the face of the waters, and God said, 'Let there be light.' And there was light."

Back at Mission Control, Jerry Bostick and others fell silent. "I've never seen this place so quiet," he said. "It was a big hush in here, and [there were] tears in a lot of eyes. It was just the perfect thing to do at the perfect time."

Lovell continued the reading. "And God called the light Day, and the darkness he called Night." And sure enough, viewers could see the boundary between sunlight and darkness on the moon's jagged surface.

Borman finished the reading, adding a final thought, "From the crew of Apollo 8, we close with good night, good luck, a Merry Christmas, and God bless all of you—all of you on the good Earth."

The TV signal went silent. Susan Borman had been watching with friends. When it was over, they went outside to look up at the crescent moon. And though it was late, Marilyn Lovell took her children on a walk through the neighborhood, its sidewalks lined with luminarias.

In a year that had seen so much violence—the escalating war in Vietnam and the assassinations of Martin Luther King and Bobby Kennedy—the message from Apollo 8 was welcome indeed.

The Trip Back

Up on Apollo 8, the crew didn't have any time to reflect. The capsule would make one more orbit before heading home.

Bill Anders said the far side of the moon "looks like a sand pile my kids have been playing in for a long time. It's all beat up." *Courtesy of NASA, AS8-12-2192*

After the kids were in bed, Valerie Anders walked over to the Borman house. She and Susan listened to the squawk box sitting together in the kitchen. As before, the SPS engine would be fired on the far side of the moon—203 seconds—while the capsule was out of radio contact.

Everyone waited. It was just past midnight in Houston, Christmas morning.

After 40 minutes of radio silence, CapCom Mattingly called the spacecraft. "Apollo 8, Houston." He repeated it four more times. And then the screens at Mission Control started lighting up. They had a signal!

"Houston, Apollo 8, over." It was Jim Lovell.

"Hello, Apollo 8. Loud and clear," replied Mattingly.

"Roger. Please be informed, there is a Santa Claus," Lovell announced.

"That's affirmative," said Mattingly. "You are the best ones to know." The burn was perfect.

Susan Borman, Marilyn Lovell, and Valerie Anders could now get some sleep.

They didn't get much—it was Christmas morning, after all. The Anders children tore into their presents, which had been delivered by a neighbor dressed as Santa. Marilyn Lovell was watching her children play when a delivery arrived. It was a large box wrapped in blue and silver foil. A spacecraft and two Styrofoam balls, one painted like the Earth and the other the moon, were attached with wire. She read the card: To Marilyn. Merry Christmas with Love, From the Man in the Moon. It was a mink coat, and although it was a warm day, she wore it to church that morning.

Up on Apollo 8, the astronauts opened their food locker and found three packages tied with red and green ribbons. Turkey and gravy, stuffing, and cranberry-apple sauce, and three small bottles of brandy from Deke Slayton. They didn't drink them, on Borman's orders. There were also small gifts from their families—cufflinks and tie tacks.

The astronauts were in good spirits on the trip back. When they weren't busy, Mission Control played Christmas carols over the radio. Lovell sang along. "I kept thinking of Jules Verne," he recalled. "When I was a boy, his books fascinated me. I never dreamed that I would one day relive one."

Back Home

James Holliday was a pilot for Pan Am Airways. On December 27 he was flying across the Pacific Ocean near the splashdown zone for Apollo 8. An hour before sunrise he spotted a dull red spot in

Apollo 8 reenters Earth's atmosphere, photographed by a US Air Force tracking plane. *Courtesy of NASA, S69-15592*

the sky. As it turned orange, he told passengers to look out the left side of the plane.

"The orange color changed to dark yellow, and a tail became visible—a comet tail," he remembered. "And all of this material remained in the sky; it didn't just die out. . . . This long trail of color ran from dark red to pink to orange to yellow, with an incandescent light up at the front, which was the capsule." And then it just snuffed out.

Inside the capsule, the astronauts were on a roller-coaster ride that no other human had ever taken. They entered the atmosphere at 24,500 mph and, as they slowed, reached almost 7 Gs, crushing their bodies down into their couches. Anders watched chunks of burning heat shield blow past the windows. At one point the capsule rotated and headed back up on a "double skip trajectory," then plummeted again.

About six miles over the ocean, the drogue parachutes opened to slow their fall, followed by the three main chutes. "When the main chutes opened it felt as if the spacecraft had just been hit by a giant fist," said Borman.

They finally hit the ocean and turned upside down in the five-foot waves. Water poured in through a vent, dousing Borman. But then the uprighting bags inflated, and the capsule turned back over.

A recovery helicopter hovered overhead, waiting for sunrise before dropping its divers into the shark-filled waters. "Hey, Apollo 8," the pilot radioed. "Is the moon made of Limburger cheese?"

"No," Anders responded, "It's made of *American* cheese!"

After the sun came up, the men were lifted into the helicopter and flown to the USS *Yorktown*. Sailors cheered as the three men walked down a red carpet, then went below to meet with doctors.

Telegrams poured in from world leaders, as well as one from 10 Soviet cosmonauts who praised the crew for "the precision of your joint work and your courage." President Johnson received a message signed by Soviet president Nikolai Podgorny: "Accept, Mr. President, our congratulations on the successful completion of the flight of the Apollo 8 spacecraft around the moon."

But it was an anonymous telegram that Borman appreciated most: "To the crew of Apollo 8. Thank you. You saved 1968."

Apollo 9

Even after Apollo 8, NASA still had plenty to learn before it could land on the moon. The lunar module (LM) had never flown with humans aboard. Astronauts had never docked the CSM and LM outside of a simulator. And the moon suit's portable life-supporting backpack hadn't been used in space.

To make testing easier, Apollo 9 would stay in Earth orbit. If the crew ran into problems, they could return quickly. However, they could not return to Earth in the LM. It was designed to land on the moon and had no heat shield. If astronauts in the LM had problems, they would need to return to the CSM before coming home.

Jim McDivitt was commander on Apollo 9, and Dave Scott was the CSM pilot. Both had flown on

Courtesy of NASA, S69-18569

Gemini. Rusty Schweickart, who had never been in space, was named the LM pilot. This crew had trained together for nearly three years. They were Apollo 1's backup crew and had been preparing for this flight since the accident.

Schweickart was excited. "The first flight of any vehicle is a test pilot's dream," he said. He and McDivitt were comfortable flying experimental aircraft—sturdy, heavy, powerful aircraft. But the LM was none of those things. It had to be light, so its walls were thin and its legs were skinny. The men were shocked the first time they saw it.

"I looked at Rusty and he looked at me, and we said, 'Oh my God! We're actually going to fly something like this?'" McDivitt recalled. "It was like cellophane and tin foil put together with Scotch tape and staples!" The crew named the LM *Spider* and the CSM *Gumdrop*.

Apollo 9 launched on March 3, 1969. During takeoff, the LM was carried behind the CSM. Once in orbit, the CSM detached from the third stage, turned around, and flew back nose first. There it docked with the LM, then pulled it out and away from the third stage. NASA called this "transposition, docking, and extraction." The third stage then fired its engine, fell back through the atmosphere, and burned up. On this flight, everything went as planned.

Space Sickness

On the third day of the mission, Rusty Schweickart felt nauseated. When he tried to wiggle into his space suit, he threw up. Luckily, he didn't have his helmet on.

The crew of Apollo 9 (l to r): Jim McDivitt, Dave Scott, and Rusty Schweickart. *Courtesy of NASA, S68-56621*

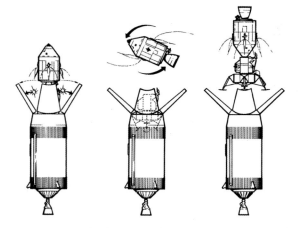

Transposition, docking, and extraction. *Adapted from Apollo Logistics Training Manual (North American Aviation, 1965), author's collection*

"If you barf in weightlessness in a space suit, you die," he later explained. "It's that simple, because you can't get that sticky stuff away from your mouth. It doesn't go down into the suit; it just floats right there and you have no way of getting it away from your nose or your mouth so that you can breathe."

Schweickart had been putting on the suit to move into the LM. Commander McDivitt postponed anything that would require that he put on his helmet. He hoped the "space sickness" would pass before the next day's EVA.

By evening, Schweickart wasn't feeling any better. *Are we going to have to actually abort the mission?* he wondered as he tried to sleep. *Is this basically a wasted mission because I'm barfing?* "That's about the lowest point in my life," he later admitted. "I had a real possibility in my mind at the time of being *the* cause of missing Kennedy's challenge of going to the moon and back by the end of the decade." Luckily, by morning Schweickart was feeling better.

The goal of Apollo 9's first EVA was to test the LM when it depressurized, as well as the moon suit. On Gemini EVAs, the astronaut was connected to the spacecraft by an umbilical line, but the Apollo moon suit had a backpack called a portable life-support system (PLSS). On the surface of the moon, the crew could walk around without getting tangled in lines leading back to the lander.

Another EVA goal was to see whether an astronaut could move from the LM to the CSM, *outside*. During the test, Schweickart would exit the LM, attached only by a 25-foot nylon rope, then crawl

Thin Skin

"I don't know if you've ever seen a tissue-paper spacecraft before, but this thing sure looks the part," said Jim McDivitt after he first saw the lunar lander. It was true—some of the LM's aluminum walls were 5/1000ths of an inch thick. This activity will give you an idea how thin that is.

YOU'LL NEED

- ☾ Empty wide-mouth jar
- ☾ Aluminum foil
- ☾ Heavy rubber band
- ☾ Pencil or pen

1. Aluminum foil can have different thicknesses. If you have "heavy duty" foil, tear off five pieces, each large enough to cover the top of an empty wide-mouth jar. If you have regular foil, tear off eight sheets.

2. One at a time, cover the top of the jar and wrap it tightly around the neck. Repeat until you've used all the sheets.

3. Wrap a heavy rubber band around the jar's neck to hold the foil in place.

4. Gently tap on the foil with your finger. Does it break through? Tap a little harder. Would you feel safe with only this much aluminum separating you from the vacuum of space?

5. Now see if you can puncture a hole in the foil using a pencil or pen. How difficult was it? (During construction, a technician once punctured an LM's wall when he dropped a screwdriver.)

over to the open CSM hatch. Knowing the motion could make Schweickart sick again, McDivitt decided Scott and Schweickart would only stand and photograph one another from their two open hatches.

Midway through the EVA, Scott's camera jammed. "OK, Dave, you got five minutes [to fix the problem]," said McDivitt. "Rusty, don't go anywhere. Just stay right there."

What an opportunity! No checklists. No tasks. Just hang out and enjoy the view. Schweickart let one hand go, turned around, and watched the Earth roll by. *My job right now is to just be a human being, just be a person*, he thought.

At first Schweickart tried to identify familiar landmarks—Rome, Greece, North Africa. But then he daydreamed. *Who am I? How did I get here?*

And he realized, *I'm here because I'm lucky. . . . I was born at the right time, went to the right school, by chance.* In later years, he realized he was witnessing humankind's evolution. "[Because of] the space program when we're off to other planets, we're off to other worlds, different atmospheres, different gravity, weightlessness, people, kids being born in weightlessness," he'd say. "Who knows what is coming?" And Schweickart understood it was his duty to share what he'd experienced with the rest of humanity.

Flying Free

On March 7 it was time to test *Spider*. McDivitt and Schweickart crawled through the docking tunnel and into the LM. With the hatches sealed, it disconnected from the CSM and slowly backed away.

The two spacecraft spent about an hour flying together while the crew double- and triple-checked *Spider*'s systems. Dave Scott observed the LM as it rotated, watching for damage or anything strange. If there was a problem, they could redock.

Once confident that the LM was fine, McDivitt and Schweickart fired its descent engine—the engine that would guide future missions down to the moon's surface—and moved away from the CSM.

During the six-and-a-half-hour flight, *Spider* flew as far as 111 miles from *Gumdrop*. About halfway through the flight, the astronauts separated LM's ascent module (the top half) from the descent module, just as it would during liftoff from the moon.

Dave Scott standing in the open hatch of *Gumdrop*, Apollo 9's CSM, docked with the LM, *Spider*, March 6, 1969. *Courtesy of NASA, AS9-20-3064*

McDivitt and Schweickart expected it to be noisy. "We figured we're not going to be able to hear each other. . . . We worked out a whole bunch of hand signals that would allow us to communicate in case something went wrong," Schweickart recalled. "So we count down, three, two, one, ignition, light off the ascent engine, and there's no noise, no noise at all. Jim and I [wondered], *What's going on?* . . . We had to look at the instrument to see that the acceleration was up, so we knew the engine was working, but it didn't make any noise at all."

McDivitt used *Spider*'s ascent engine to return to *Gumdrop*. As the LM approached the CSM, Scott radioed, "You're the biggest, friendliest, funniest-looking spider I've ever seen."

After docking, Apollo 9 stayed in orbit another five days to test the spacecraft's tracking and navigation systems. The mission ended on March 13. The capsule splashed down 180 miles northeast of Puerto Rico and was recovered by the USS *Guadalcanal*.

Because of his space sickness, Rusty Schweickart became a test subject. "I figured part of my job at that point was to help NASA to learn as much as possible about motion sickness," he said. "I became the guinea pig, the poking, the pincushion that people stuffed their pins in and their probes in and whatnot."

Apollo 10, the Dress Rehearsal

No Apollo crew was as experienced as the three astronauts on Apollo 10. The commander, Tom

Spider on its first solo voyage, orbiting the Earth, March 7, 1969. *Courtesy of NASA, AS9-21-3212*

Stafford, had flown in space twice. So had John Young, the CSM pilot. And Gene Cernan, the LM pilot, had been on one Gemini mission.

Apollo 10 would be the first chance to test both the CSM and the LM in lunar orbit, where they would be out of contact with Mission Control much of the time. "There are too many unknowns up there," Stafford explained. "Our job is to eliminate as many of them as we can, and the only way we can do that is to take the thing down to nine miles or less and see how it behaves that close to the moon." Apollo 10 was NASA's dress rehearsal.

Apollo 10 lifted off from Pad 39B on May 18, 1969. The Saturn V rattled the crew in their harnesses more violently than any had felt on their Gemini flights, and they saw a giant fireball outside the capsule when the rocket's second stage ignited.

THE LUNAR MODULE

The Apollo lunar module was a miracle of engineering. Like the CSM, the LM (pronounced "lem") had two main parts. The lower half, the **descent module**, held the spacecraft's five-ton **descent engine**. It was a variable thrust engine, meaning it could fire strongly or softly depending on what was needed. The descent stage stood 10½ feet tall, including its four legs. A 5-foot-long **contact probe** hung from each landing pad and would signal when the LM reached the surface. Experimental equipment, tools, and (in later flights) the lunar rover, were stored inside the descent module. It was wrapped in gold Mylar to reflect the sun's harsh rays.

The astronauts rode in the upper half of the LM, the 12-foot-tall **ascent module**. It held the spacecraft's computers, instruments, **antennae**, and life-support systems. To maneuver in space, the crew fired its four thrusters, called **RCS engines**, located around the cabin. The astronauts flew the LM standing up—it had no seats.

The LM was a fragile vehicle. The cabin walls and three **windows** were so thin they bulged when the cabin was pressurized. On Earth, the legs would collapse if the LM was fully loaded with fuel but could support its one-sixth weight on the moon's surface.

After landing on the moon, the astronauts would crawl backward through the square **main hatch** onto a platform called the **porch**, then down the ladder to the surface. (There was also a round **docking hatch** on top, used to move between the LM and CSM when docked.) When it was time to leave the moon, the ascent module broke off from the descent module, pushed upward by an **ascent engine**.

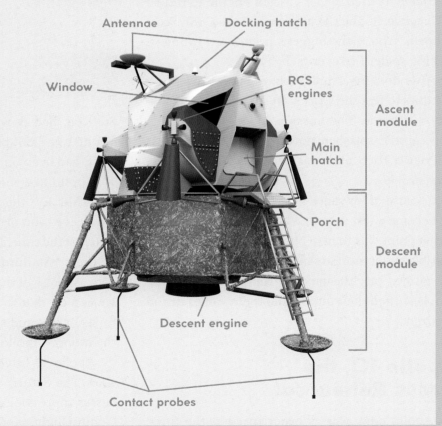

123RF.com, © nerthuz

"Are you sure we didn't lose *Snoopy* on that staging?" Cernan asked Mission Control. (The crew named the LM *Snoopy* and the CSM *Charlie Brown*.)

"No, I think *Snoopy* is still there with you," CapCom Charlie Duke radioed back. "You're looking good."

After one and a half orbits, Stafford fired the stage-three engine to head off to the moon. Apollo 10 was over Australia at the time, and citizens in Sydney saw a bright greenish light appear in the night sky and then shoot off.

"We're on the way," Stafford said. But as they accelerated, the spacecraft began to screech and groan. Soon it was shaking so strongly they could barely read the instrument panel.

"OK, we're getting a little bit of high-frequency vibrations in the cabin. Nothing to worry about," Stafford reported in his smooth Oklahoma drawl. *No way*, he thought, his gloved hand tightly gripping the abort handle. *We've come this far—if she blows, then she blows.* Six minutes later, the engine shut down on schedule. Everything was fine.

Apollo 10 was on its way to the moon. TV viewers watched as the CSM undocked from the third stage, turned around, and pulled the LM free—live in color. Once *Snoopy* was extracted, the broadcast ended.

"Only now did we finally get a chance to catch our breath and take a look back," Stafford recalled. "Blue and white, the size of a basketball, earth was . . . shrinking before our eyes. For the first and only time in my space flights, I felt strange. It was a long, long way from the windmill on that farm near May, Oklahoma."

"We Are Close, Babe"

While coasting to the moon, Gene Cernan opened the tunnel to the LM and found its insulation had disintegrated. Tiny flecks of white fiberglass floated everywhere. Worried they might clog the spacecraft's air vents, the crew chased and sucked up the pieces with a small vacuum.

Apollo 10 reached the moon on May 21. Flying around the far side, they fired the CSM's engine and entered orbit. "Well, now that we're here, what do we do?" Young joked.

Cernan remembered what they did first: "We became like three monkeys in a cage, scrambling to the windows to get a close look at this big gray thing turning below us."

Courtesy of NASA, S69-31959

The crew of Apollo 10 (l to r): Gene Cernan, John Young, and Tom Stafford. *Courtesy of NASA, S68-42906*

(left) **Apollo 10's mascots, Charlie Brown and Snoopy, at Mission Control.** *Courtesy of NASA, S69-34314*

(right) **Photo of the moon's surface taken by Apollo 10.** *Courtesy of NASA, AS10-32-4823*

Apollo 10 circled the moon nine times, taking photos and checking out the spacecraft's systems, before Stafford and Cernan closed the hatch on the LM and undocked.

"Have a good time while we're gone, babe," Cernan told Young.

"Don't get lonesome out there, John," Stafford added.

Young wasn't concerned. He finally had room to move around. "You'll never know how big this thing is when there's only one guy in it," he said.

Stafford fired *Snoopy*'s descent engine and the LM dropped toward the moon. The spacecraft reached its lowest point—47,000 feet, about 8.9 miles—over the Sea of Tranquility. This is where Apollo 11 hoped to land.

On their first pass over the site, Stafford said, "There's enough boulders around here to fill up Galveston Bay." But also, "The surface actually looks very smooth, like a very wet clay, but smooth, with the exception of the big craters."

Cernan sounded more excited. "We're right there! We're right over it!" he radioed. "I'm telling you, we are low, we are close, babe. This is it!"

Snoopy flew over the moonscape for almost eight hours taking hundreds of detailed photos. Then it was time to return to *Charlie Brown*. "I just wish we could stay," Stafford admitted.

Before *Snoopy* could return, Stafford would have to drop the LM's bottom half—the descent module—and fire its ascent engine. Just before he did, the lander began tumbling out of control.

"We're in trouble!" Stafford called out. He took over control from the computer, then hit the switch that dumped the descent module. This helped, but *Snoopy* somersaulted eight times before Stafford could steady it, just in time to fire the ascent engine.

"Something went wild there," Stafford calmly reported. "We're all set."

Mission Control listened helplessly throughout the ordeal, as did millions on television. NASA later determined that a switch had been left in the wrong position—a human error.

Two hours later the LM and CSM rendezvoused as they passed behind the moon. When they reemerged, Stafford announced, "*Snoopy* and *Charlie Brown* are hugging each other."

"We Know We Can Go to the Moon"

Charlie Brown orbited the moon for another day, taking photos. The crew also studied the moon's mascons—mass concentrations—that made its gravity uneven. These heavy remnants of enormous metallic meteorites could change the altitude of an orbiting spacecraft by as much as two miles, which made rendezvous and navigation tricky.

After 31 orbits, they were ready to return. An hour after transearth injection, Cernan told TV viewers, "You've often heard of the nursery rhyme about the man in the moon. We didn't see one there . . . pretty soon we hope that there [will be] two men on the moon."

Charlie Brown splashed down near Pago Pago on May 26, 1969. Soon the crew was greeted by clapping sailors as they exited the recovery helicopter. "After days in zero G, we were so wobbly that each step along the pitching carrier deck was a little adventure," Cernan admitted.

One hour after splashdown, NASA administrator Thomas Paine spoke to reporters. "Eight years ago yesterday, the United States made the decision to land men on the moon and return them safely by the end of the decade," he began. "Today, this moment, with the Apollo 10 crew safely aboard the USS *Princeton*, we know we can go to the moon. We *will* go to the moon. Tom Stafford, John Young, and Gene Cernan have given us the final confidence to make this bold step."

The flight controllers in Houston had already hung up a sign in Mission Control: 51 DAYS TO LAUNCH. At Kennedy Space Center, Apollo 11 sat ready on Pad 39A. The Saturn V had been rolled out while Apollo 10 was on the way to the moon.

(left) **An artist's depiction of** *Snoopy* **firing its descent engine.** *Courtesy of NASA, S69-33765*

(below) ***Charlie Brown*, as seen from** *Snoopy*, **May 22, 1969.** *Courtesy of NASA, AS10-27-3873*

The *Eagle* Has Landed

The countdown for Apollo 11 started at 8:00 PM on July 10, 1969, six days before liftoff. As crews prepared and inspected the Saturn V and Apollo spacecraft, spectators began arriving in Florida.

"We were at Cocoa Beach a week ahead of the actual launch day and people were already gathering," recalled Geneva Barnes, who worked at NASA. "The evening before launch there were people sleeping on the beaches and in their cars because there were no more hotel rooms. Some spent the night sitting in chairs in hotel lobbies. The motel and restaurant marquees at Cocoa Beach were all saying, GOOD LUCK APOLLO 11."

Spectators at the launch of Apollo 11: Vice President Spiro Agnew (green suit) and former president Lyndon Johnson (blue suit), July 16, 1969.
Courtesy of NASA, 107-KSC-69PC-379

Among the estimated one million spectators at the Cape were 20,000 special guests, including former president Lyndon Johnson and hundreds of senators, representatives, and other politicians, as well as 3,500 journalists from around the world. Half a billion viewers followed on TV. The only place not crawling with people was Pad 39A. It was normally bustling with workers, so Mike Collins was surprised at how empty and quiet it was when the crew arrived.

Commander Neil Armstrong was the first astronaut loaded in, followed by Collins. As Buzz Aldrin waited, he looked out into the distance. "As far as I could see there were people and cars lining the beaches and highways. The surf was just beginning to rise out of an azure-blue ocean. I could see the massiveness of the Saturn V rocket below and the magnificent precision of the Apollo capsule above," he later wrote. "I savored the wait and marked the minutes in my mind as something I would always want to remember."

"You're It"

On January 6, 1969, Deke Slayton asked Neil Armstrong, Buzz Aldrin, and Mike Collins to come to his office. With the door closed, he said, "You're it, guys." Apollo 11 would land on the moon, and they would be the crew. The three men quietly accepted the assignment, stood up, and shook hands.

That afternoon, Joan Aldrin picked up Buzz from work in their station wagon. The family's washing machine had broken, and she had baskets of dirty laundry in the backseat. As they drove to a laundromat, her husband told her the news.

"Buzz went to work this morning without a job and came home tonight LM pilot on Apollo 11, the first lunar landing. So it is really happening and I am scared," she wrote in her diary. The thought made her so nervous that a week later she broke out in hives, admitting only in her diary, "I wish Buzz were a carpenter, a truck driver, a scientist, anything but what he is."

Armstrong, Aldrin, and Collins were the perfect crew for Apollo 11—calm, intelligent, and experienced. But they acted more like coworkers

The Apollo 11 crew (l to r): Neil Armstrong, Mike Collins, and Buzz Aldrin. *Courtesy of NASA, S69-31739*

than close friends. When they came to the launch-pad for tests, they would drive up separately. When they ate lunch, each sat alone.

NASA suggested the crew choose more majestic names for the spacecraft than *Snoopy* or *Gumdrop*. They settled on *Columbia*, a name once used for the "New World." The lander would be *Eagle*.

Launch Day

The Apollo 11 crew moved to Cape Kennedy one month before the launch. Some questioned if they could finish their training in time. So many things could go wrong on a mission—the crew had to know how to handle them all. There was even talk of delaying the launch.

But they didn't have much time. NASA had only a few months left to meet Kennedy's challenge. And the Soviet Union? It had one last moon plan of its own: the N-1 rocket.

The N-1 was Russia's version of the Saturn V, a rocket strong enough to send a crew to the moon. It was first tested on February 21, 1969. Two of its 30 first-stage engines unexpectedly shut down after launch. Soon, all the rest failed. The rocket exploded about 17 miles away.

The second N-1 launched on July 3, two weeks ahead of Apollo 11. The unmanned rocket took off at 11:00 PM, rose just 600 feet, then fell back toward the pad before exploding in a giant purple fireball. Flaming rubble and molten metal rained down on the Baikonur Cosmodrome, seriously damaging the facility. Russia's hope of beating America to the moon came to an abrupt end.

Google the Moon

Google hasn't just mapped the Earth—it's mapped the moon. Each of the six Apollo landings has been documented in detail in much the same way the homes on your block have.

Start by pulling up www.google.com/moon/ on your computer. Click on the Apollo 11 icon to find it on the labeled map. Zoom in on the site until you see a set of numbered tags. These are important locations from *Eagle*'s time on the surface—where the astronauts planted the flag, where they set up the scientific experiments, where they took important photos. If you click on a tag, a brief description of what happened there will pop up. As you read about the astronauts' EVA on the moon, find the tags related to their activities.

Bookmark this website and refer to it as you read about later Apollo missions. It will help you better understand how the astronauts explored the moon.

As Apollo 11's launch approached, Dee O'Hara, the astronauts' nurse, chatted with Armstrong. "You will not believe the number of people that have congregated down here," she said. "The causeways are jammed. They've been out there for a week. It's just this mass of people."

"Well, yeah, I suppose people are going to make a big deal out of this," he laughed.

O'Hara was startled. "Neil, do you realize what you've just said?"

"Yes, it's no big deal." he replied.

"Well, maybe not to you," O'Hara replied, "but it certainly is to the rest of us."

The astronauts spent their final day on Earth relaxing at a beach cottage south of the launchpad. Buzz Aldrin searched for coins and other treasures in the sand with a metal detector.

And then it was July 16: launch day. The crew ate breakfast, had brief medical exams, and got into their space suits. Their pockets held pencils, flashlights, handkerchiefs, and scissors to cut

Apollo 11 heads for the moon, July 16, 1969. Courtesy of NASA, 69PC-0421

wire. Armstrong also stashed a comb and a packet of candy.

After a 20-minute ride to the pad, they rode the elevator to the White Room outside the capsule. Armstrong handed a slip of paper to Guenter Wendt. It was a SPACE TAXI TICKET that read, GOOD BETWEEN ANY TWO PLANETS. The crew was loaded in and the technicians left.

At 9:32 AM, the engines fired. "Liftoff! We have a liftoff, thirty-two minutes past the hour. Liftoff on Apollo 11," reported announcer Jack King, his voice cracking with emotion. He wasn't alone. Many of the spectators at Cape Kennedy were crying as the rocket shot through the clouds and disappeared into the distance. Science fiction writer Arthur C. Clarke cried too. "This is the last day of the Old World," he said.

"The *Eagle* Has Landed"

Joan Aldrin had planned to clean house as her husband flew to the moon, to keep her mind off the mission. Instead, she spent every day listening to the squawk box. Dozens of reporters prowled outside her home. If she had to leave, friends would sneak her away in the backseats of their cars, covered with blankets.

Nothing unusual happened on the three-day journey to the moon. On July 19 the spacecraft slipped into orbit, and the crew prepared for the big day.

President Nixon declared July 20, 1969, a "National Day of Participation." Though most Americans weren't working anyway—it was a

Casting Shadows

The Apollo landings were all timed to provide the best possible conditions for the astronauts to see what they were doing. If the sun was directly overhead at their landing site, it could be difficult to spot craters and boulders. Apollo 11 landed when the sun was just 10 degrees above the horizon. Just like during a sunrise or sunset on Earth, the angle of the sunlight would create long shadows. On an all-white moonscape, this was important. This activity will show you why.

YOU'LL NEED

- Sheet of blank, white paper
- White rice
- Flashlight
- Short cardboard tube (toilet paper)
- Dark room

1. Place a sheet of white paper on a table in front of you. Scatter a few grains of rice on the paper.

2. Turn on a flashlight and turn off the room lights.

3. Holding a short cardboard tube to your eye, look directly down at the paper.

4. Shine the flashlight down at the rice and paper from directly above. How easy is it to see the rice?

5. While continuing to look at the paper, move the flashlight down and to the side, always keeping it shining on the rice. Can you see the rice better now?

6. Imagine this is the surface of the moon, and the grains of rice are boulders. Where would you want the sun to be during landing?

Sunday—he encouraged bosses to let their employees stay home to watch the landing.

In Houston, Gene Kranz started the day by getting a fresh flattop haircut and putting on the new white vest that his wife, Marta, had sewn. Before his team reported for its shift at Mission Control, Kranz listened to several John Philip Sousa marches in his office. (He did this every morning.)

After eating breakfast, all three astronauts suited up. Armstrong and Aldrin made last-minute checks of the LM, and Collins sealed the tunnel between the two spacecraft.

On the 13th orbit, the LM disconnected from the CM. The ships flew together for a while. Collins watched the LM slowly spin around as he looked for any damage to the lander. "I think you've got a fine looking machine there, *Eagle*, despite the fact you're upside down," he said.

"Somebody's upside down," replied Armstrong.

"You guys take care," said Collins.

"See you later," Armstrong radioed back, and the two spacecraft moved apart.

Mission Control gave Armstrong the OK to descend to 50,000 feet. The LM would make one final pass behind the moon, dropping lower and lower, and when it came back around, it would be time to land.

With *Eagle* out of radio contact, Gene Kranz ordered Mission Control to take a five-minute break. Everyone rushed to the bathroom. After they'd returned, Kranz spoke privately to his team. "Today is our day, and the hopes and the dreams of the entire world are with us," he said. "In the next hour we will do something that has

never been done before. . . . The risks are high—that is the nature of our work. You are a hell of a good team, one that I feel privileged to lead. Whatever happens, I will stand behind every call that you will make."

Kranz then ordered the doors to the control room locked—nobody would be allowed in or out until *Eagle* was safely on the moon's surface, or the landing was called off. Or they crashed.

Everyone waited.

As soon as the LM reappeared on radar, it disappeared. Radio contact cut in and out, and Mission Control had to decide if a landing was possible.

Then a flood of data came through from *Eagle*. Kranz polled his team, Go or No Go for PDI—powered descent initiation—the last step before landing. All said Go.

CapCom Charlie Duke gulped. "*Eagle* . . . you're Go for PDI." Armstrong and Aldrin fired the descent engine. As it came up to full power, the LM began to shake and rattle.

Eagle drifted along, dropping lower by the second. Armstrong realized they were passing over key landmarks two seconds earlier than expected. If this continued, they'd overshoot the landing site. Then, as they passed 33,000 feet, a yellow alarm button flashed.

"Program alarm. It's a twelve-oh-two," Armstrong reported. Kranz couldn't recall what a 1202 alarm was, but guidance officer Steve Bales did: the guidance computer was overloaded.

The LM continued down while Bales looked for a solution. The 26-year-old computer expert had just 15 seconds to decide what to do. The guidance

program was written to restart if overloaded, so unless the light stayed on, the ship was fine.

"We're Go on that alarm," said Bales. *Eagle* kept going.

As the lander passed 7,000 feet, Armstrong could see the computer was taking *Eagle* down into a crater. He switched to manual control—he would pilot the LM himself.

"You are Go for landing," CapCom Duke radioed.

"Roger, understand. Go for landing," Aldrin replied, and then almost immediately, "3,000 feet. Program alarm. 1201."

"We're Go on that alarm," Bales shouted. Duke told Aldrin to ignore it.

At 1,000 feet, Armstrong saw boulders, then another crater.

"Sixty seconds," Duke said. Just a minute of fuel left.

Armstrong kept looking, passing over yet another crater. Then he spotted a flat clearing.

Kranz called to Charlie Duke, "You'd better remind them there ain't no damn gas stations on the moon." But Deke Slayton was sitting next to Duke and punched him in the side.

"Charlie, shut up. Let them land."

Joan Aldrin clung to the frame of her living room door. The house was filled with family and friends, all glued to the TV.

Mission Control held its breath. *Eagle* dropped lower, the engine blowing up clouds of dust.

"30 seconds," Duke warned.

"Contact light!" Buzz Aldrin said—the sensors hanging from *Eagle*'s landing pads had touched

MARGARET HAMILTON, SOFTWARE PIONEER

Apollo 11 landed on the moon using computer code developed by Margaret Hamilton. As director of the Software Engineering Division at MIT's Draper Lab, she devised a way for the computer to prioritize its tasks, and to do the important tasks first. When the *Eagle*'s alarms rang, the overloaded computer automatically went back to recalculate its guidance numbers, rather than shut down altogether.

Asked later about the first landing, Hamilton said, "I was so happy, but I was more happy about [the software] working than about the fact that we landed." The software was updated for the later flights to work even better.

Hamilton was awarded NASA's Exceptional Space Act Award in 2003, which acknowledged, "The Apollo flight software Ms. Hamilton and her team developed was truly a pioneering effort." In 2016 she was honored with the Presidential Medal of Freedom.

Margaret Hamilton and a printout of the computer code for the Apollo spacecraft, 1969. *Draper Laboratory, courtesy of Wikimedia Commons*

THE MOON SUIT

The Apollo moon suit was a remarkable spacecraft all its own. It weighed 183 pounds on Earth, but only 30 pounds on the moon. An astronaut would put it on in pieces, like a knight with a suit of armor. First, against the skin, the astronaut wore a medical harness that would monitor his heart rate and other bodily functions and transmit the information back to doctors on Earth. Over that, the astronaut wore a **liquid cooling garment**, or LCG. (The liquid was water.) It looked like long underwear but had 300 feet of tubing woven into the fabric to keep the astronaut comfortable. This was important, because the moon's surface temperature could go from -250°F in the shade to 280°F in the sun.

On top of everything was the main **pressure suit**. There were 21 different layers of fabric to protect the astronaut from heat, cold, radiation, air leaks, and even micrometeoroids. When fully pressurized in the vacuum of space, it was difficult to bend at the waist, elbows, and knees. That is why photos of the astronauts often show their arms up in front of them.

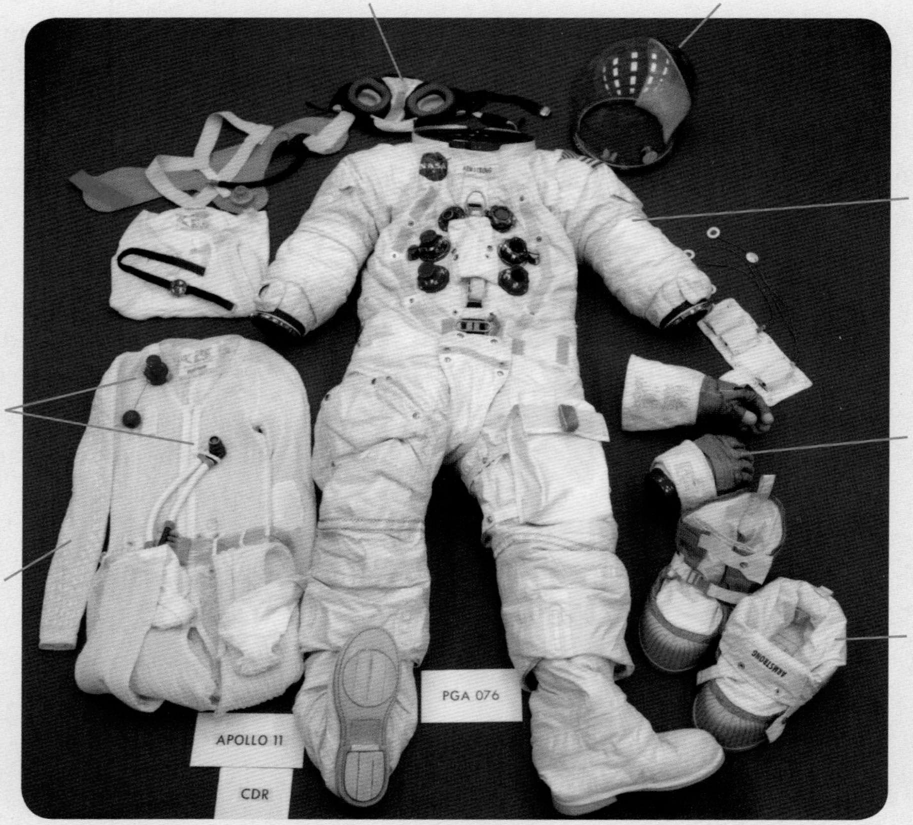

Communications cap

Helmet

Pressure suit

Gloves

Hose attachments (blue in, red out)

Liquid cooling garment (LCG)

Lunar overshoes

Courtesy of NASA, S69-38889

PGA 076

APOLLO 11

CDR

Thick **gloves** slipped over the wearer's hands and attached to metal wrist rings. The gloves were not very flexible, and closing a hand was like squeezing a tennis ball. Astronauts wore clunky **lunar overshoes** over their moon-suit shoes to help them walk in the dust.

Each suit was attached to a portable life-support system, a large backpack that pumped the water in the undergarment, oxygen, communication equipment, and an emergency oxygen backup system. The PLSS was connected to the suit through **hoses** that connected in the front.

The clear bubble **helmet** was made from polycarbonate, 30 times stronger than Plexiglas. It had a gold see-through visor that could be pulled down to protect the astronaut from the sun's harsh rays. Each astronaut also wore a **communications cap**, which they called a Snoopy cap, that held their microphone and earphones in place.

The moon suits were made by the International Latex Corporation, the same company that manufactures Playtex bras and underwear.

the surface. Armstrong hit the Engine Stop button and LM settled onto the moon, so softly that neither astronaut felt it hit.

"We copy you down, *Eagle*," radioed Duke.

For three very long seconds, nobody responded. Then came Armstrong's voice: "Houston, Tranquility Base, here. The *Eagle* has landed."

"Roger, Twang . . ." the tongue-tied Duke began. "*Tranquility*, we copy you on the ground. You got a bunch of guys about to turn blue. We're breathing again. Thanks a lot."

Joan Aldrin collapsed to the floor, then rose and staggered to another room to compose herself. Dee O'Hara had been watching the landing with Aldrin. "I kept shaking my head," she recalled. "I thought, this can't be real, it just can't be. Here we are, on another planet. It was goose bumps all around."

Mission Control, which had erupted in cheers, quickly got back to work. They had to be ready if *Eagle* needed to leave in an emergency.

One Giant Leap

July 20 had been a quiet afternoon at the Two Guys gas station in Downey, California. Sixteen-year-old Mike Pohlen had heard that Apollo 11 had landed and hoped to get home before the astronauts' moonwalk. His shift ended at 6:00 PM, and driving home he turned onto Firestone Boulevard, the main street in town.

"You could have rolled a bowling ball from one end to the other and not hit a thing," he recalled. "There wasn't another car in sight!"

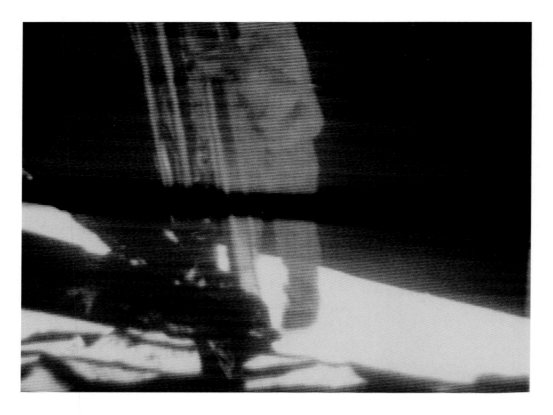

Millions watched Neil Armstrong descend Apollo 11's ladder to make the first steps on the moon, July 20, 1969. Armstrong's crewmate, Mike Collins, missed it because *Columbia* was on the far side of the moon at that moment. *Courtesy of NASA, S69-42583*

"Everyone forgot, for a few moments, that we were all citizens of different countries on Earth," recalled Soviet cosmonaut Alexei Leonov. "That moment really united the human race. Even in the military center where I stood, where military men were observing the achievements of our rival superpower, there was loud applause."

The original plan was for Armstrong and Aldrin to eat and rest before heading out onto the moonscape, but who could take a four-hour nap? Armstrong requested to move up the planned EVA, and Mission Control agreed.

After eating, Armstrong and Aldrin began the long process of suiting up for their moonwalk. "It was very cramped in the *Eagle*," recalled Aldrin. "We felt like two fullbacks trying to change positions inside a Cub Scout pup tent."

With their suits on, they depressurized the cabin. It took longer than expected. Just enough pressure remained in the cabin to keep the hatch from opening. Finally, Aldrin gently peeled back a corner of the hatch and it popped open with a spray of ice crystals.

Armstrong got down on his hands and knees and backed out through the opening. At the top of the ladder he pulled a ring and a TV camera turned on. Viewers on Earth saw a fuzzy black-and-white image of . . . *something*. It wasn't clear.

Armstrong described every move as he slowly descended the ladder, then dropped the final three feet onto the landing pad.

Just one more step. What would he say?

People had been asking Armstrong this same question for months, including astronaut Bruce

Like so many who lived in Downey, Pohlen's father worked at the North American Rockwell plant where the Apollo CM was built. When he got home he found the family gathered around the television, waiting for the moonwalk to begin. His father had pulled his chair up close and was grinning from ear to ear.

And it wasn't just Downey. Around the world, 600 million humans watched and waited. Tens of thousands went to New York's Central Park to see it unfold live on screens set up by CBS News. Even criminals took a break—there was a 90 percent drop in crime worldwide the night of the moonwalk.

McCandless, who would be the CapCom during the moonwalk. Armstrong said, "I'll probably just say something like, 'Boy, it sure is dusty up here. OK, here we go. . . . There's a rock.'"

But now it was time—10:56 PM in Houston, more than six hours after landing. McCandless kept quiet so he wouldn't spoil the moment.

Armstrong raised his left foot from the landing pad and planted his boot in the dust.

"That's one small step for man, one giant leap for mankind."

Armstrong moved slowly at first, holding on to the LM like a toddler as he tested the one-sixth gravity. Then, after letting go, he scooped up a "contingency sample" of lunar soil, put it in a bag, and shoved it into a pocket on his moon suit. If *Eagle* had to leave in an emergency, at least scientists would get something.

Nineteen minutes later, Aldrin crawled out onto the porch. "I want to back up and partially close the hatch, making sure not to lock it on my way out," he said.

"A pretty good thought," Armstrong laughed.

Aldrin descended the ladder and stood on the pad. "Beautiful view!" he said.

"Isn't that something!" replied Armstrong.

Stepping into the dust, Aldrin said, "Magnificent desolation."

Once they were comfortable walking—which was more like hopping—the pair got to work. First: raise the American flag. It wasn't easy—as hard as they pushed, they could only get the flagpole six inches into the lunar soil. Armstrong later said it was the mission's scariest moment, that the flag might tumble over. Armstrong took a quick photo of Aldrin saluting it.

Before Aldrin could get a shot of Armstrong doing the same, Mission Control broke in. President Nixon was calling.

"Neil and Buzz! I am talking to you by telephone from the Oval Room at the White House, and this certainly has to be the most historic telephone call ever made," Nixon said. "Because of what you have done, the heavens have become a part of man's world. And as you talk to us from the Sea of Tranquility, it inspires us to redouble our efforts to bring peace and tranquility to Earth." He ended by wishing them a safe trip home.

There was awkward silence—the radio signal took 1.3 seconds to get there, and 1.3 seconds back. At last Armstrong replied, "Thank you, Mr. President. It's a great honor and privilege for us to be here representing not only the United States but men of peace of all nations."

And then it was back to work. They could spend a little over two hours outside the LM, and they had already used 53 minutes. Armstrong loaded a large "bulk sample" of rocks and lunar soil into an aluminum case while Aldrin began unloading scientific equipment.

The crew set up three main experiments: a solar wind detector, a seismometer, and a reflector to measure the distance to Earth. The solar wind detector was a long, aluminum sheet that collected atoms of argon, helium, krypton, neon, and xenon emitted from the sun. The seismometer would measure vibrations in the moon's crust. And the reflector had 100 prisms that could bounce back

Buzz Aldrin on the moon. Neil Armstrong can be seen in the visor's reflection, July 20, 1969. *Courtesy of NASA, AS11-40-5903*

laser signals sent from Earth to determine how far away the moon was at any moment. It was accurate to six inches.

The astronauts spent the rest of their time collecting rocks. Unlike earlier samples, these rocks were carefully selected, described, and placed in labeled bags.

Both astronauts snapped photos as they went about their work—339 shots between them. Armstrong took many of Aldrin, but Aldrin only took two of Armstrong. Armstrong ended up taking the clearest photo of himself . . . a small reflection in Aldrin's visor.

Soon, they returned to the lander. The astronauts had explored an area about the size of a

baseball infield. They left behind an Apollo 1 mission patch given to them by Gus Grissom's son, and a gold pin of an olive branch, symbolizing peace. They also left two small medallions honoring cosmonauts Yuri Gagarin and Vladimir Komarov, who had also perished in the space race, and a silicon disc imprinted with goodwill messages from 73 world leaders.

Aldrin reentered the LM first and brought in the boxes of samples. As Armstrong looked up, he noticed that with his arm extended he could block out the Earth with his thumb. Later he was asked if it made him feel big. "No," he replied. "It made me feel really, really small."

Armstrong then hopped onto the ladder, leaving footprints that will remain on the moon for centuries to come. The astronauts also left garbage that will probably be there even longer— they tossed out their boots, backpacks, empty food containers, and full urine bags.

Once *Eagle* was repressurized, the astronauts took off their helmets. Because their suits were coated with dust, they could now tell what the moon smelled like: wet ashes and burnt gunpowder, like the odor of a firecracker.

The men then noticed a big problem: while exiting the lander, Aldrin had knocked off the switch that armed the ascent engine. If they couldn't repair it, they wouldn't be able to leave the moon. Aldrin suggested jamming a felt-tip pen into the empty hole, and it worked.

The men ate and got some rest before heading home. The LM was cold, cramped, and uncomfortable, and the bright reflection of the Earth shined

One of the only color photos of Neil Armstrong on the moon, standing in the *Eagle*'s shadow, July 20, 1969. *Courtesy of NASA, AS11-40-5886*

through the windows. Armstrong slept just three hours, Aldrin four.

Heading Home

While his crewmates slept in the LM, Mike Collins did the same in the orbiting CM. Collins admitted that he would have liked to have gone to the surface, but he was happy to have played a part in this grand adventure.

The CM orbited every two hours, and for almost half of that—48 minutes—he was behind the moon, completely cut off from Mission Control and the *Eagle*. Still, he wasn't lonely. The silence was a nice break from the constant radio chatter. It gave him rare moments to reflect. "I thought a lot about my family," he said, "but beyond that I thought about the planet Earth and what a magnificent place to live it is, and how tranquil it looks from a great distance."

Twenty-one hours after they landed—not even a full day—Armstrong and Aldrin were set to head home. They fired the explosive bolts that separated the ascent module from the bottom half of the lander and the ascent engine rocketed them upward, like a high-speed elevator. The blast from the engine blew down the flag they had so carefully set up.

It took just over three hours to rendezvous with *Columbia*. As Armstrong slowly maneuvered to dock, Mike Collins snapped a photo of the ship with the Earth in the distance. "I realized that for the first time, in one frame, appeared three billion earthlings, two explorers, and one moon,"

LUNA 15

While Armstrong and Aldrin were asleep after their EVA, the Soviet Union tried once more to beat the Americans. Overhead, the unmanned Luna 15 probe was preparing to land on the lunar surface, drill a core sample, and return to Earth before Apollo 11. NASA knew it was coming and had even traded information with the Russians to be sure the two spacecraft didn't collide in orbit.

The plan failed. The Soviets did not have good maps of the surface. Luna 15 slammed into the side of a mountain near the Sea of Crises, 700 miles northeast of Apollo at the Sea of Tranquility.

he later wrote. "The photographer, of course, was discreetly out of view."

Collins opened the hatches between the LM and CM after docking. Aldrin came through first, then Armstrong, the men smiling and laughing and shaking hands. They then transferred the boxes of rock samples. "I handled them as if they were absolutely jam-packed with rare jewels, which in a sense they were," recalled Collins.

With everything aboard the CM, they left the LM behind. *Columbia* detached from *Eagle* and Mission Control used its thrusters to nudge the empty module on a gentle path back to the moon. Collins noticed that his crewmates looked sad as it moved away. Several weeks later it crashed on the lunar surface.

Assemble a Personal Preference Kit

When the Eagle *landed on the moon, it carried a number of remarkable items. Neil Armstrong brought a piece of fabric and a sliver of wood from the Wright brothers' first flyer. Buzz Aldrin brought two booklets by Robert Goddard, one of which he later gave to Goddard's widow.*

These were part of the astronauts' personal preference kits (PPKs). Each Apollo astronaut was allowed to bring along a small ½-pound bag of items—souvenirs for family and friends. "I carried prayers, poems, medallions, coins, flags, envelopes, brooches, tie pins, insignia, cuff links, rings, and even one diaper pin," wrote Mike Collins.

If you were going to the moon, what would you put in your PPK?

YOU'LL NEED

◐ Kitchen scale

◐ Resealable bag

◐ Personal items

1. Select a number of personal items you would put in your PPK. These can be small objects that are important to you, your family, or friends.

2. Starting with your favorite item, place each on a kitchen scale until you reach the ½-pound limit.

3. Were you able to include everything in your PPK? If not, is there something heavy you can remove to replace with smaller and lighter items?

4. Once finished, place your items in a resealable plastic bag. Was it as much as you expected?

Replica of the gold olive branch left by Neil Armstrong on the moon, July 20, 1969. *Courtesy of NASA, 71-HC-602*

The flight back was uneventful. The astronauts listened to music on tape. Armstrong brought a recording of Antonín Dvořák's *New World Symphony* and a strange album by Dr. Samuel Hoffman called *Music Out of the Moon*. The tape also had sound effects—a freight train, barking dogs, and bells—which they played over the radio to confuse Mission Control.

Quarantine

On July 24 the Apollo 11 command module splashed down in the Pacific Ocean one minute early. A helicopter dropped three divers into the water. They opened the hatch and tossed in three biological isolation garments, or BIGs, and closed the capsule again. The BIGs—sealed coveralls with helmets and breathing filters—would keep any possible "moon germs" from escaping as the astronauts were moved to the USS *Hornet*.

Once zipped up, the crew opened the hatch again and jumped into a life raft. They then scrubbed each other with chemical detergent before being lifted, one at a time, into the waiting helicopter.

At the ship, the crew was quickly moved into a special trailer called the mobile quarantine facility (MQF). The astronauts took a quick shower, shaved, and put on clean blue jumpsuits. President Nixon was there to welcome them back.

(left) **The *Eagle* ascent stage returning to *Columbia*, July 21, 1969.** *Courtesy of NASA, AS11-44-6642*

(right) **The Apollo 11 crew in their BIGs after splashdown, July 24, 1969.** *Courtesy of NASA, 108-KSC-69PC-452*

All three men squeezed together to peer out the MQF's small window, where the president stood at a microphone.

Nixon congratulated them and invited them to visit the White House after they were released. "This is the greatest week in the history of the world since the Creation," he said. "As a result of what you've done, the world has never been closer together before."

The Apollo crew would be isolated for three weeks. Three days after splashdown, the *Hornet* sailed into Pearl Harbor, Hawaii. The MQF was loaded onto a flatbed trailer and paraded through Honolulu past an ocean of cheering citizens. One young boy ran alongside the MQF for several miles. It was then flown to Houston, where it

arrived in the middle of the night to even larger crowds, and the crew's waiting families.

"Welcome home!" Pat Collins shouted into the phone. "You look great!"

Buzz Aldrin asked his son Andy how school was going. Andy reminded him, "Daddy, it's summer vacation."

At last the MQF reached the Manned Spaceflight Center where the crew moved into a large sealed facility called the Lunar Receiving Laboratory (LRL). It had 20 rooms, including living quarters, a library, a dining room, and meeting rooms. Inside, germ-free animals—mice, birds, fish, shrimp, quail, cockroaches, and oysters—were exposed to the moon rocks and dust to see if they would come down with some unknown space sickness. Armstrong, Aldrin, and Collins were given dozens of medical tests, and seemed fine.

During their containment, they wrote detailed mission reports and were interviewed by NASA staff. They also relaxed, played ping-pong and gin rummy, and autographed thousands of photos. Armstrong, who turned 39 while in quarantine, practiced strumming his ukulele.

International Heroes

Armstrong, Aldrin, and Collins were released on August 10, 1969. Three days later, four million people welcomed them at a ticker-tape parade in New York City. They addressed the United Nations, then were whisked off to Chicago for another parade. The day ended with a banquet in Los Angeles, the Apollo 11 Moon Ball. President

Still isolated in the MQF, the Apollo 11 astronauts are reunited with their wives in Houston, July 27, 1969. *Courtesy of NASA, S69-40147*

Nixon awarded each man with the Medal of Freedom, and a fourth medal was presented to computer whiz Steve Bales, for Mission Control.

On September 29 the crew and their wives embarked on the Giantstep–Apollo 11 Presidential Goodwill Tour. The first stop was Mexico City. "We landed . . . and went from the airport into town. The roads leading into the city were jammed with people," recalled Julian Scheer, who organized the trip. "One of the first handwritten signs we saw was held by someone who had leaned out the window. . . . It read, 'Apollo 11 Astronauts—This Is Your Home.' We all saw it at the same time, and it struck us as a great sentiment. . . . The landing had indeed captured the imagination of the world."

During the 45-day tour, they visited 23 different countries on every continent except Antarctica. They ate state dinners with presidents, prime ministers, kings and queens, and Pope Paul VI. Between 100 and 150 million people turned out to see them firsthand.

The attention was overwhelming. After returning to Houston, Joan Aldrin wrote in her diary, "The tinsel is tarnished. Buzz, who was never comfortable with all this, pushes loyally on. I cooperate, but I am tired and unhappy." Mike Collins knew the toll his work had taken on his family, and asked Deke Slayton to take his name out of consideration for future flights. Over the coming years, Neil Armstrong gave fewer and fewer speeches, and eventually stopped signing autographs. None of the men ever returned to space.

The Apollo 11 astronauts on a parade through Mexico City, September 29, 1969. *Courtesy of NASA, 70-H-1553*

Apollo 12 and the Go-Go Crew

Pete Conrad, Dick Gordon, and Alan Bean—Pete, Dickie-Dickie, and Beano—the fun-loving "Go-Go Crew." Residents in Cocoa Beach would see them in their powder blue flight suits and aviator glasses, racing around town in matching gold Corvettes.

Conrad and Gordon had been friends since serving together in the navy and had flown together on Gemini 11. "Pete and I could communicate

89

The Apollo 12 crew (l to r): Pete Conrad, Dick Gordon, and Alan Bean. *Courtesy of NASA, S69-38852*

Courtesy of NASA, S69-52336

however, anticipated what would happen during launch.

It was raining on November 14, 1969, the day Apollo 12 was set to lift off. If the Saturn V didn't launch, the crew would have had to wait another 28 days. President Nixon had come to Florida to watch. It was just a little rain—no sign of lightning for 19 miles. The countdown continued.

At 4:22 PM, the Saturn V lifted off the pad. At 6,000 feet, just 36 seconds later, the rocket was hit by lightning. "What the hell was that?" said Gordon as the capsule shuddered. Warning lights flashed all over the control panel.

Sixteen seconds later, Apollo 12 was struck again.

"OK, we just lost the [guidance] platform, gang. I don't know what happened here—we had everything in the world drop out," radioed Conrad.

Back at Mission Control, Flight Director Gerry Griffin turned to 24-year-old John Aaron, who was monitoring the rocket's electrical systems. Aaron's computer screen was a mess of nonsensical numbers.

"Flight, try S-C-E to Aux," Aaron said. This meant, *Switch the system to another plug.* The Cap-Com radioed Bean, who flipped the switch. Aaron's computer screen blinked, and now showed numbers—good numbers.

By this time, the rocket had punched through the clouds and was only moments from first-stage separation.

WHAM! The men were jolted in their harnesses when the Saturn's first stage broke away and the second stage ignited.

without talking," said Gordon. "We trusted each other. We thought alike." Then Bean joined the pair after Clifton "C. C." Williams, Apollo 12's original LM pilot, died in a plane crash near Tallahassee, Florida.

Apollo 12 was the first all-navy crew, so they named their spacecraft after ships: *Yankee Clipper* for the CM and *Intrepid* for the LM. The mission was scheduled to launch 16 weeks after Apollo 11, allowing NASA to modify the flight plan based on what they'd learned on the earlier flight. Nobody,

The rocket seemed fine, but the CSM's three fuel cells appeared to be dead. Houston told Bean to reboot them one at a time. One by one, they returned to normal.

But was everything OK? "We were afraid we may have fried something so badly that we jeopardized the mission. So . . . we took an extra revolution in Earth orbit," said Griffin. "That gave us a little more time. We . . . checked out everything we could in the rear end on the service module." Everything was working.

Mission Control gave the crew permission to leave Earth orbit. Dick Gordon fired the third-stage booster and off they went.

Pinpoint Landing

Compared to the launch, Apollo 12's trip to the moon was boring. "There wasn't a lot to do other than shave and brush your teeth," Conrad joked. They also spent time boogieing in zero gravity to the song "Sugar, Sugar," which Bean had brought along on a cassette tape.

After arriving at the moon on November 18, the crew slept before heading to the surface. The mission's main goal was to land within walking distance of Surveyor 3, which had landed on the moon two and a half years earlier. The astronauts would remove parts from the spacecraft and bring them back for study.

The next morning, Conrad and Bean moved into the lander. In the final moments before closing the hatch between the CSM and the LM, Gordon teased Conrad. "Let's go over it again, Pete: the gas is on the right, the brake is on the left." The men laughed, and then Gordon got serious, "Go get me some rocks, partner."

"See ya tomorrow, Dickie-Dickie," said Conrad.

The *Intrepid* leaves the *Yankee Clipper* to land on the moon, November 19, 1969. *Courtesy of NASA, AS12-51-7507*

Bean looked back through the tunnel at Gordon and thought, *Will I ever see this guy again? Wonder what's going to happen to us? I hope I see him in a few days.*

Though Bean's official title was lunar module pilot, it was the commander—Conrad—who piloted the LM. Bean would monitor the lander's instruments and feed Conrad with important information as they descended.

The computer guided the *Intrepid* most of the way down. At 7,000 feet, Pete Conrad peered out the window looking for his target: "Pete's Parking Lot."

"Hey, there it is—there it is!" he exclaimed. "Son of a gun, right down the middle of the road!"

Bean quickly glanced at the approaching surface. Craters were everywhere. "Wow, this is scary," he mumbled. Then he returned to his instruments. "Looks good out there, babe. Looks good."

The closer they got, Conrad could see that Pete's Parking Lot was covered in boulders. He switched the *Intrepid* to manual control and banked sharply to the left, aiming for a smooth patch. Then, hovering at 200 feet, they started their final descent, straight down.

Dust blew out in all directions. "I couldn't see our landing area at all from 100 feet on down," Conrad recalled. "It was just one big gray blanket below us."

Down, down, through the billowing dust . . .

"Thirty feet," Bean announced. "You got plenty of gas. Plenty of gas, babe."

The blue CONTACT light popped on, and Conrad punched the ENGINE STOP button. *Intrepid* fell the last foot and hit with a thud.

"Good landing, Pete! Outstanding, man!" Bean told the laughing Conrad.

Dick Gordon, orbiting above, radioed his crewmates. "Congratulations from *Yankee Clipper!*" he said. "Have a ball."

"Whoopie!"

Italian journalist Oriana Fallaci refused to believe that Neil Armstrong had come up with his famous first line on the moon. "One small step . . ." The whole world was watching—NASA wouldn't just leave it up to the astronaut. Never!

She was arguing with her friend, Pete Conrad, who just happened to be the next astronaut scheduled to land on the moon.

"Look, I'll prove it to you," Conrad replied, and came up with what he'd say when he stepped off the lander. It was so goofy, she had to know *he* had come up with it, not some writer at NASA. And Conrad bet her $500 to make it interesting.

And now, at the foot of the ladder, Conrad was going to win that bet. "Whoopie! Man, that may have been a small one for Neil, but that's a long one for me!" he said.

Conrad slowly stepped back away from the ladder and looked around. "Boy, you'll never believe it. Guess what I see sitting on the side of the crater?"

"The old Surveyor, right?" Bean guessed.

"The old Surveyor. Yes, sir," said Conrad. "Does that look neat! It can't be any further than 600 feet from here." He'd done it—a pinpoint landing.

Conrad went directly to work collecting a contingency soil sample. "Dum dee dum dum dum," Conrad sang as he hopped around.

Now it was Bean's turn to crawl out of *Intrepid*. Once on the moon, he hopped over to the crater to see Surveyor 3 for himself. At the rim, he reached into a pocket of his moon suit, pulled out his silver astronaut pin, and tossed it into the wide hole. He knew he'd be getting a gold pin when he returned.

Mission Control and TV viewers watched all of this live, in color. But not for long. While moving the lander's camera, Bean accidentally pointed it directly at the sun. The intense sunlight fried it. So much for live TV from the moon.

Apollo 12 had two scheduled EVAs. The crew set up the Apollo lunar surface experiments package (ALSEP) in the first EVA. It had experiments to detect solar wind, measure moonquakes, monitor the moon's magnetic field, and more.

The ALSEP was powered by a rod of plutonium, which Bean had to install. "Everything was going great on the surface until I tried to transfer the nuclear fuel element from its carrying cask into the generator," he said later. "[But] the element wouldn't budge. . . . We used the only tool available, the hammer. Pete beat on the side of the cask and I pulled. . . . He pounded so hard that he fractured the graphite case. . . . The case was about 1,400° Fahrenheit and I was surprised that I

could feel the heat through my suit." With enough whacks, they finally got it out.

After almost four hours outside, Conrad and Bean returned to *Intrepid* for lunch and to rest. Bean had requested spaghetti because Bean *loved* spaghetti. "Like most 'space food' in those days, it tasted pretty bland. But I didn't care much about that. I had told my children, Clay and Amy, that their dad was going to be the first man to eat spaghetti on the moon. And I was."

Alan Bean descends from the *Intrepid*, **November 19, 1969.** *Courtesy of NASA, AS12-46-6726*

Space Art

There has long been a mystery surrounding a stowaway on Apollo 12: a ½-by-¾-inch ceramic wafer created by sculptor Forrest Myers titled Moon Museum. *The white chip had drawings by six famous artists imprinted on it—Myers, Andy Warhol, Claes Oldenburg, Robert Rauschenberg, David Novros, and John Chamberlain. Myers asked NASA to send it to the moon. When they refused, he got a technician to hide it under the gold Mylar foil wrapped around the lander's legs. Or so he claimed. No technician ever admitted to hiding the artwork.*

If you could send a "museum" to the moon, what would you put on it?

YOU'LL NEED

- Scrap paper
- White cardstock
- Ruler
- Scissors
- Fine-tip markers

1. On scrap paper, sketch out a work of art for your "moon museum." It should be simple, because you will be re-creating it small.
2. With a ruler, measure out a ½-by-¾-inch rectangle on the corner of a sheet of cardstock.
3. Cut out the rectangle.
4. Transfer your design onto the cardstock using fine-tip markers.
5. Does your "moon museum" look the way you imagined? Make another if you want changes.
6. It's up to you to figure out how to sneak it onto a spacecraft.

Bonus: Both Warhol and Rauschenberg did famous artworks with Apollo themes. Research online to find Rauschenberg's Saturn V lithograph, *Hot Shot*, and Warhol's Buzz Aldrin portraits, titled *Moon Walk*.

Back on Earth, the three TV networks scrambled to figure out what to do after losing the video signal—viewers were tuning out. For the second EVA, CBS and ABC had actors in moon suits to recreate the astronauts' movements on a fake moonscape while Conrad and Bean's voices played live. NBC used marionettes instead of actors. The show was so well done, some viewers didn't realize they were watching a puppet show.

During the second EVA, the astronauts trekked down into the crater to Surveyor 3. They photographed it first. It was tan, as if it had baked in the sun. They then used bolt cutters to remove metal tubing, the scoop, and the camera. Engineers back on Earth would study it all to determine the long-term effects of space on spacecraft. For the rest of the EVA, they collected rocks.

Finally, it was time to return to the LM. Bean went in first. Then Conrad saluted his father, who had died a month earlier, before climbing the ladder a final time.

Take It for a Spin

Dick Gordon would have enjoyed going to the moon's surface with his friends. But he took his role as CM pilot seriously. "I had a job and a function to perform," he said. "I was happy for them." Besides, being alone in *Yankee Clipper* wasn't so bad. "You don't have to worry about anybody else. . . . There's a lot of things that you have to do and accomplish. And it's a moment of solitude," he said later. "When the sun shines on the moon . . .

Alan Bean holds a soil sample container during the second EVA of Apollo 12, November 20, 1969. *Courtesy of NASA, AS12-49-7278*

there are features that you can look at and see that you hadn't seen before." Once asked if he ever got frightened, all alone a quarter of a million miles from home, Gordon just shrugged. "Well, I don't know, you've got the whole universe outside your window."

He wasn't alone long. Thirty-two hours after landing, *Intrepid* was headed back. It would take two hours to rendezvous, and since Conrad was flying the spacecraft, Bean looked out the window at the moonscape below.

The Apollo 12 crew during recovery, November 24, 1969. *Courtesy of NASA, S69-22265*

On their final orbit behind the moon, Conrad surprised Bean, "Would you like to fly this thing?" Bean said Mission Control would freak out. "Don't worry about it. We're behind the moon—they can't tell what we're doing," laughed Conrad. So Bean took the controls and maneuvered *Intrepid* left, then right, and up and down. Nothing big. But to Bean, it was one of the kindest things anyone had ever done for him.

After a few minutes, Conrad took back control and guided *Intrepid* through docking with the *Yankee Clipper*. When Dick Gordon opened the hatch

linking the two spacecraft, all he saw was a cloud of black dust. He slammed the hatch back shut.

"Dick, what the hell?" shouted Conrad.

"You're not coming in my ship like that, Pete," replied Gordon.

He was serious. Gordon passed down two storage bags for their filthy moon suits and ordered them to strip—everything. They finally came through, naked as the day they were born.

After stowing the rocks and gear, they undocked from *Intrepid* and sent it back toward the moon. When it crashed on the surface, the

ALSEP's seismometer recorded the impact. The crust vibrated for 30 minutes, like a bell.

Four days later, Dick Gordon piloted *Yankee Clipper* back through the atmosphere, watching the heat shield burn away during reentry. "As the heat builds, the colors . . . it's kind of a corkscrew out there behind you," he said. "There's yellows and reds and greens and purples and they're all mixed up." The capsule splashed down just three miles from the USS *Hornet*—another pinpoint landing.

The crew was placed in quarantine, but only for 16 days. On December 10 the astronauts were released to their happy families. In the months that followed, Bean would go to a local mall, buy ice cream, and sit and watch the people go by. *Wasn't it wonderful they were all alive at this moment in history?* he pondered.

NASA had met Kennedy's challenge . . . twice! The astronauts and ground support were making a trip to the moon and back look easy. That would soon change.

The crew of Apollo 12 arrive in Houston, still quarantined inside the MQF, November 29, 1969. *Courtesy of NASA, S69-60644*

"Houston, We've Had a Problem"

Two days after launching on April 11, 1970, Apollo 13 was scheduled for a TV broadcast. The astronauts were almost 200,000 miles from Earth, one day from the moon.

The television networks weren't interested in another episode of floating food and "tours" of the tiny spacecraft. Instead, they stuck to their regular programming. Marilyn Lovell had to pack up her four kids and drive over to Mission Control, where they could watch the show from the VIP gallery. Mary Haise, wife of rookie astronaut Fred Haise, and the couple's three children joined them. She was seven months pregnant at the time.

The broadcast lasted 31 minutes. Jim Lovell ended saying, "This is the crew of Apollo 13 wishing everybody there a nice evening, and we're just

Mission Control during the Apollo 13 television broadcast, just moments before the explosion, April 13, 1970. Fred Haise is on-screen, Gene Kranz sits with his back to the camera. *Courtesy of NASA, S70-35139*

about ready to close out our inspection of *Aquarius* and get back for a pleasant evening in *Odyssey*. Goodnight." (*Aquarius* was their name for the LM; *Odyssey* was the CM.)

The Lovells and the Haises then drove home. Flight controllers had a few final requests. "Thirteen, we've got one more item for you when you get a chance: we'd like you to stir up your cryo tanks," radioed CapCom Jack Lousma.

"OK, stand by," said Jack Swigert, the CM pilot.

The command module had several super-cooled storage tanks filled with liquid oxygen and hydrogen, and if they weren't stirred once in a while, the contents became a "thick soupy vapor" and wouldn't work as well. Stirring was done by flipping a switch.

Two minutes later, there was a dull bang and the spacecraft shook.

Lovell looked to Haise, then Swigert. Neither had any idea what had happened.

"I believe we've had a problem here," Swigert reported.

The CapCom asked Swigert to clarify.

Lovell came on the radio. "Houston, we've had a problem."

Controller George Bliss looked at the numbers on his computer screen. The command module's no. 2 oxygen tank appeared to be gone. Vanished. That tank held half the crew's breathable oxygen. "We've got more than a problem," he said.

Down in the Trench, the name given to Mission Control's rows of computer monitors, the controllers watched "the command module's life-sustaining resources disappearing, like blood draining from a body," Gene Kranz recalled. "The controllers felt they were toppling into an abyss."

Apollo 13, "From the Moon, Knowledge"

Apollo 13 was going to be the first science mission. Every Apollo mission to this point had focused on how to get to the moon—the technical challenge. But Apollo 13 had a full schedule of experiments to perform. It even had "science" right on its mission insignia: *Ex Luna Scientia*. "From the Moon, Knowledge."

Deke Slayton selected Jim Lovell to command the flight. Lovell would become the first US astronaut to fly a fourth space mission. Two rookies filled out the crew: Ken Mattingly would pilot the CM and Fred Haise the LM.

Preparations had been going well until a few weeks before launch. Then astronaut Charlie Duke got the measles. Duke contracted the disease from one of his son's playmates. NASA doctors were alarmed. German measles are highly contagious, and Duke, who was on the Apollo 13 backup crew, had been in all the same offices, simulators, and lunchrooms as the prime crew. There wasn't a vaccine at the time. The only way to avoid the measles was to have already had them. Lovell and Haise had the measles as children, but not Ken Mattingly.

NASA couldn't risk having an astronaut sick a quarter-million miles from Earth, so they made the decision to pull Mattingly off the flight. Jack Swigert, the backup CM pilot, was moved on to the crew.

Courtesy of NASA, S69-60662

Problems like this were the reason Apollo had backup crews in the first place. Swigert had been training for this mission all along. Still, Lovell and Mission Control needed to be convinced that this very-last-minute change would work. As soon as NASA learned of Duke's condition, Swigert was put into the simulators with Lovell and Haise. After three long days, they were convinced.

A change like this would normally have been big news, but it came out the same day the Beatles announced that they were breaking up. The following afternoon, Apollo 13 lifted off from Pad 39A. Far fewer reporters covered the launch, and once the Saturn V disappeared from view, TV stations returned to their regular programs.

During the flight out, Jack Swigert realized he'd forgotten to file his income taxes. He radioed Mission Control to ask how to get an extension. That was the biggest problem during the first two days. CapCom Joe Kerwin admitted to the crew, "We're bored to tears down here."

What Now?

"When that accident happened, I don't think anybody at first recognized the severity of it," flight director Gerry Griffin recalled. "People were still saying, 'Well, we can't land if we don't do so and so and so and so.'"

But not for long. Back at *Odyssey*, Fred Haise scanned the instrument panel. "[It] became very clear in short order . . . that the pressure meter, the temperature, and the quantity meter needles for one of the oxygen tanks was down in the

The Apollo 13 crew (l to r): Jim Lovell, Jack Swigert, and Fred Haise. *Courtesy of NASA, S70-36485*

bottom of their gauges." Looking out the window, Lovell and Haise saw a sea of debris and a cloud of . . . *something*. They thought they'd been hit by a meteor.

Odyssey was quickly losing power. Electricity in the CSM was generated by three fuel cells. Liquid oxygen and hydrogen mixed inside them to create water and electricity. Now, half of the CSM's oxygen supply was gone, and nobody knew what else had been damaged when the tank exploded.

Haise tried to switch the power line to a different fuel cell but found it dead as well. Only one fuel cell was still working, and it was fading fast.

The gas spewing out the side of the service module was pushing *Odyssey* and *Aquarius* around, and the guidance computer was trying to stop the movement by firing the ship's thrusters. The linked spacecraft creaked and groaned as they vibrated uncontrollably.

Apollo 13 had already passed the point of equigravisphere and was now being pulled toward the moon, faster and faster. To get back to Earth, the crew would have to swing out around the moon first. But they couldn't worry about that just yet.

"We figure we've got about 15 minutes' worth of power left in the command module," the CapCom reported, "so we want you to start getting over in the LM." The crew had only one option: shut down the CSM and move over into the undamaged lunar lander. *Aquarius* would be their lifeboat.

Jim Lovell quickly transferred the navigation information they needed to the LM, and—ready or not—Swigert turned off the CSM. Would they even be able to turn on *Odyssey*'s power when they got back to Earth? They'd just have to figure that out later.

Back at Mission Control, Gene Kranz gathered his best controllers for a meeting. This "Tiger Team" had three main challenges. First, they had to figure out how to get the LM, which was designed to keep two men alive for two days, to keep three men alive for four days. Second, they had to get the crippled spacecraft on a path back to Earth. And finally, they had to come up with a way to restart the CSM when it returned to Earth and fly it back through the atmosphere. There would be thousands of crucial decisions over the days to come, and they couldn't be indecisive.

Kranz ended by telling the team, "When you leave this room, you must leave believing that *this crew is coming home*. I don't give a damn about the odds, and I don't give a damn that we've never done anything like this before. Flight control will *never* lose an American in space. You've got to believe, your people have got to believe, that this crew is coming home. Now let's get going!"

A Team Effort

"Within minutes, people started pouring in [to Mission Control] from all over," Ken Mattingly remembered. "The next shift, people that weren't on shift. . . . Within an hour, the center looked like daylight. Everyone that had ever given a

Flight controllers and astronauts working together to save Apollo 13, April 14, 1970.
Courtesy of NASA, S70-34986

thought to Apollo was there. . . . *We'll bring 'em home.*"

In the days to come, Ken Mattingly, Gene Cernan, Joe Engle, and other astronauts would all but live inside the Apollo simulators, testing out new procedures before Mission Control sent instructions to Lovell. Other astronauts stayed with the crew's families to explain what they were hearing on their squawk boxes and to relay updates from Mission Control.

To get home, Apollo 13 had to get itself on a "free-return trajectory." Traveling through space is a bit like miniature golf—if you hit a ball just so, in precisely the right direction, it'll curve over the bumps and off the walls for a hole in one. On its current path, Apollo 13 would slingshot around the moon and back toward Earth but miss it by 45,000 miles. The crew needed to fire an engine that would nudge them onto a perfect path—the free-return trajectory.

With *Odyssey* dead, the only engine left was the descent engine on *Aquarius*. It was designed to get the lander down to the moon, not push a broken command module through space. But what choice did they have?

Mission Control calculated that a 31-second burn of *Aquarius's* engine, five and a half hours after the explosion, would do the trick. At 2:42 AM, Houston time, Lovell fired the descent engine as the LM's guidance computer kept the spacecraft headed in the right direction.

And it worked! Sixteen hours later, Apollo 13 swung around the far side of the moon. Haise and Swigert scrambled to take photos. Lovell warned them not to waste time, but they pointed out that he'd been to the moon before. They hadn't. So for a few moments, Lovell joined them at the windows.

Two hours after emerging from behind the moon, at 8:40 PM on April 14, the crew executed a "get home maneuver" to speed up their return. They fired *Aquarius's* descent engine for four and a half minutes to increase their speed back toward Earth. The maneuver shortened the four-day trip to two and a half days.

At this point, the crew had barely slept since the explosion. Deke Slayton got on the radio. "Hey guys, this is Deke. Just wanted to let you know we're gonna get you back. Everything's looking good," he assured them. "Why don't you quit worrying and get some sleep?"

"We think that's a pretty good idea," said Lovell.

So while the crew tried to rest, Mission Control worked on a way to turn the damaged CSM back on. They hadn't yet figured it out.

Frogs in a Frozen Pond

When the Lovells' priest stopped by their home to visit with the family, 12-year-old Susan Lovell ran crying to her bedroom. Marilyn followed her daughter, then took her outside for a walk. Though she knew, she asked Susan why she was upset.

"What do you mean? I'm worried dad's not going to come home," Susan said.

Marilyn tried to reassure her, saying that her dad was "the best astronaut I know." It was about all she could say.

Up in *Aquarius*, the crew tried to sleep. It was cold and damp, like a walk-in cooler. Moisture from their breath condensed on the walls and instrument panels.

"We're three men cold as frogs in a frozen pond," Lovell reported.

The astronauts were also slowly suffocating. Each time they breathed, they added more carbon dioxide to the air. Normally, the carbon dioxide would be removed by lithium hydroxide "scrubbers." *Aquarius* only had two filter canisters, and they were cylindrical. *Odyssey* (still shut down) had more canisters, but they were square and couldn't fit into the LM's scrubber.

Back on Earth, astronaut John Young led a team to build an adaptor using items found in the spacecraft—tubing from a space suit, duct tape, the cover from a flight plan, and a sock. They called it the "mailbox" because of its shape. The crew was given instructions on how to build it, and soon clean air was flowing again through *Aquarius*.

Later that evening, Apollo 13 had to fire *Aquarius*'s descent engine a third time—just 14 seconds—to keep the spacecraft headed in the right direction. The CSM had continued to leak oxygen, and it was slowly pushing them off course.

Finally, with 19 hours until Apollo 13 would strike Earth's atmosphere, Mission Control was ready to send the crew instructions on how to restart *Odyssey*, detach the damaged service module, undock from *Aquarius*, and splash down in the Pacific. The instructions ran 39 pages long and included more than 400 steps.

CapCom Vance Brand radioed the procedure line by line to the crew. Each instruction and switch setting was written down, then repeated back to Brand to confirm that they'd heard it correctly. The process took two hours.

(left) **Jack Swigert with the square "mailbox" air filter, April 17, 1970.** *Courtesy of NASA, AS13-62-9004*

(right) **The damaged Apollo 11 service module floats away, April 17, 1970.** *Courtesy of NASA, S70-35703*

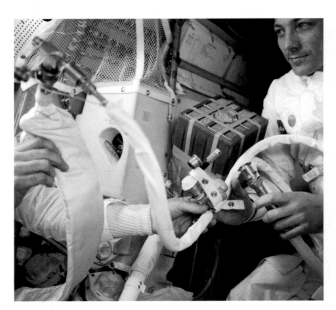

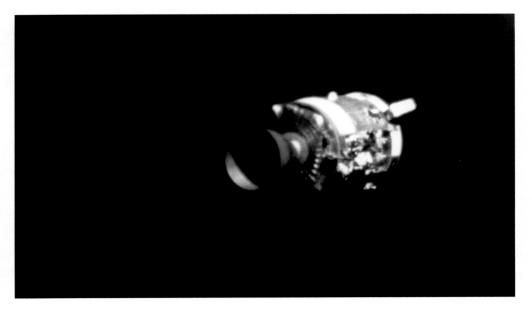

Four and a half hours before reentry, Swigert detached the service module from the command module. As it floated away, Lovell saw it through an LM window. "There's one whole side of that spacecraft missing!" he reported. "The whole panel is blown out, almost from the base of the engine!"

With little time left, the crew powered up the CM and sealed the hatch to the LM. Swigert flipped a switch, there was a bang, and the lander drifted away.

"Farewell, *Aquarius*," the CapCom said. "And we thank you."

Thousands stopped in New York's Grand Central Station to watch the live TV coverage. The pope led prayers in St. Peter's Square for the crew's safe return, as did 100,000 Hindu pilgrims in India.

Marilyn Lovell watched from the family's home in Timber Cove, along with Jim's mother, Blanch, and dozens of close friends and neighbors. Privately, NASA had told her and Mary Haise that the crew had a 10 percent chance of returning alive . . . if things went well.

In the last minutes before reentry, Swigert said, "I know all of us here want to thank all you guys down there for the very fine job you did."

Lovell agreed. "That's affirm, Joe."

"I'll tell you, we all had a good time doing it," replied CapCom Joe Kerwin.

The moment approached when Mission Control would lose radio contact. "Everyone says you're looking great," Kerwin reassured them.

Swigert's voice was the last anyone heard. "Thank you."

A Successful Failure

Gene Kranz waited almost five minutes, then turned to Joe Kerwin. "OK, Joe, give them a call."

"*Odyssey*, Houston. Standing by," the CapCom called.

Nothing.

A few seconds passed and they called again. And then again. Another minute went by in silence.

Then came word from someone in the Trench—there was a signal!

"OK, Joe," came Swigert's voice.

Live video soon showed three bright parachutes gently lowering the *Odyssey* out of the clouds. Minutes later it splashed down in the calm Pacific Ocean, just three miles from the USS *Iwo Jima*. When navy divers opened the spacecraft's hatch, a cloud of cold mist emerged, and then the astronauts. Soon they were standing on the deck of the aircraft carrier.

Together, the crew had lost 32 pounds. Fred Haise had a serious kidney infection that would lay him up for some time. But they were home.

Back in Houston, the partying in Togethersville had just begun. Marilyn Lovell spoke to reporters on her front lawn. "I have never experienced anything like this in my life, and I never hope to experience it again," she admitted. But she was smiling for the first time in three days.

The following day, President Nixon presented Gene Kranz, Glynn Lunney, and the rest of the flight controllers the Presidential Medal of Freedom. The Apollo 13 crew received the same honor when they reached Hawaii.

Jim Lovell reads the headlines aboard
the USS *Iwo Jima*, April 17, 1970.
Courtesy of NASA, S70-15501

All future Apollo flights were put on hold as NASA investigated the accident. The culprit was simple and small: the contractor that built the fuel cell had failed to replace a 28-volt thermostat on a 65-volt switch inside the tank, and it fried. With the thermostat broken, there was no way to tell that the tank was dangerously overheating.

What went *right*, however, was difficult to document. Lovell and Haise tried to re-create in the simulator some of the emergency procedures they'd taken during the flight, but they could never do it—they were too slow.

Jim Lovell later said, "Our mission was a failure, but I like to think it was a successful failure." But many in Washington saw it differently. Some lawmakers called for an end to Apollo—it was getting too risky. The Apollo 20 mission had been

axed in January. By September, Apollos 18 and 19 were canceled as well.

Apollo 14 would be a make-or-break mission. Luckily, the commander on that flight was already an American hero.

Apollo 14, the Three Rookies

Alan Shepard, the first American to fly into space, was also selected as commander of the first Gemini flight. It was scheduled to launch in early 1964. But in late 1963 Shepard went to NASA doctors when he started feeling dizzy and nauseated.

The diagnosis was devastating: Ménière's disease, which caused fluid to build up in his inner ear. Shepard was grounded in February 1964 not just from Gemini but also from flying an airplane without a copilot. Deke Slayton asked Shepard to be the head of the Astronaut Office. It was an important job managing the Gemini and Apollo crews, but a desk job nonetheless.

For some, Ménière's disease went away on its own, but not for Shepard. As time went on, he went nearly deaf in his left ear, and his balance got so bad he had trouble walking across a room without falling.

Then Shepard learned about a new experimental procedure that could reverse the problem. In the summer of 1968, he checked into a California hospital under an assumed name, Victor Poulos, to have the operation. His symptoms gradually improved, then vanished, and in March 1969 the NASA doctors declared him fit to fly.

Deke Slayton recommended that Shepard command Apollo 13. Shepard asked for Ed Mitchell and Stu Roosa join him on the crew. Neither had flown to space before, but both had impressed Slayton with their intelligence and dedication.

The news did not go over well with the rest of the astronauts, who thought Shepard was jumping ahead in line. Gordon Cooper, the only other Mercury astronaut still on Apollo, was so angry he resigned.

NASA management wasn't sure Shepard was the best pick for Apollo 13, either. He needed more training. George Mueller, head of the Office of Manned Space Flight, overruled Slayton, moving Shepard's crew to Apollo 14 and Jim Lovell's crew up to Apollo 13.

The Apollo 13 accident and the investigation that followed pushed Apollo 14 from July 1970 to January 1971. In that time, for increased safety, engineers added one more oxygen tank, a spare battery, and additional water storage to the CSM.

Stu Roosa, who would pilot the improved CSM, named it *Kitty Hawk* in honor of the Wright brothers. Ed Mitchell named the LM *Antares*, after a bright star that would be visible during the lunar landing. The crew was nicknamed "the Three Rookies," because they had just 15 minutes of spaceflight experience—combined—and that was during Project Mercury.

Problems Along the Way

Because of the German-measles incident, the Apollo 14 astronauts were put in quarantine three

The Apollo 14 crew (l to r): Stu Roosa, Alan Shepard, and Ed Mitchell. *Courtesy of NASA, S70-55387*

weeks *before* the launch. The night before liftoff, the crew and their families said their good-byes through a window at the astronauts' quarters.

Alan and Louise Shepard kissed each other at the glass pane. "I won't be making my usual phone call tomorrow night," Shepard said. "I'll be leaving town."

The following morning, January 31, 1971, Deke Slayton rode with the crew to Pad 39A. "Watch your ass and have a good trip," Slayton told his longtime Mercury friend. When Shepard got to the gangway at the top of the tower, he looked down. Slayton was still standing there, watching, and Shepard gave him the thumbs up.

"I could hear the rocket hissing and rumbling," Mitchell remembered, "and it reminded me of an

turned around, and tried to dock with *Antares*. The two spacecraft bumped, then drifted away from each other.

Roosa tried again, hitting the *Kitty Hawk* a little harder. Nothing. Shepard wondered if he'd need to put on his space suit to go out and fix the problem.

Three more docking attempts, and three more failures. Finally, Mission Control suggested Roosa keep firing his thrusters *after* the ships met, to keep them pushed against each other, and the latches finally worked. After debating whether it would be safe to undock when they got to the moon (since they would have to dock again later), NASA gave the go-ahead for landing.

Apollo 14 entered lunar orbit on February 4. Twelve orbits later, Shepard and Roosa undocked *Antares* from *Kitty Hawk* and started their descent to Fra Mauro, east of the Ocean of Storms. "It felt like being in a small boat that had been set free from a large ship in the chilling darkness of night," Mitchell wrote.

As *Antares* dropped to the surface, a bright red ABORT light came on. Ground controllers thought it was a glitch. "Ed, could you tap on the panel around the ABORT pushbutton?" the CapCom asked. Mitchell did, and the light went off. Worried that the faulty switch might create a problem as *Antares* got closer to the surface, they sent up computer instructions to hotwire the switch.

At 32,000 feet the ship's landing radar flashed warnings; it couldn't "see" the moon's surface. Mitchell was told to reboot the system. It started working at 15,000 feet, shortly before they would

enormous upright steam train waiting at the station, ready to go." The train didn't leave the station on time, however. A passing thunderstorm delayed the launch for 40 minutes.

When the Saturn V finally rose through the overcast Florida skies, the crew celebrated.

"Beautiful!" Shepard said.

"Go, baby, go!" Roosa shouted.

"She's going, she's going! Everything's good!" reported Mitchell.

All did not go well, however. A half hour after TLI, as Apollo 14 was on course to the moon, Roosa flew *Kitty Hawk* away from the third stage, have had to call off the landing. But nobody who knew Al Shepard, who was flying the LM, thought he would pass up a landing, radar or no radar. Finally, he set *Antares* down in a cloud of moon-dust just 165 feet from its target, Cone Crater.

After checking the LM's systems and getting the OK to stay from Mission Control, Mitchell asked the happy Shepard, "Just between you and me, would you have really flown us down without the radar?"

"You'll never know, Ed," Shepard winked. "You'll never know."

Lost on the Moon

After eating and suiting up, the astronauts headed outside. Shepard went first. When he reached the lunar surface, the 47-year-old commander said, "It's been a long way, but we're here."

"Not bad for an old man," the CapCom said.

Shepard backed away from the lander and looked up to see the crescent Earth. He wasn't an emotional guy, but later admitted that he got choked up.

Mitchell soon joined Shepard. "With a check-list on one arm and a watch on the other, Alan and I were constantly looking at our wrists to stay on schedule and on task," he remembered.

On this mission, the astronauts had a two-wheeled cart called a modular equipment transporter (MET), which they pulled around by hand. This "lunar rickshaw" carried their equipment, cameras, maps, and rock and soil samples. But the MET didn't work as well as hoped—it got bogged

3-D Rocks

The first three lunar landings—Apollos 11, 12, and 14—brought along a device called the Apollo lunar surface closeup camera, or ALSCC. This camera had two lenses placed a few inches apart, like your eyes. The ALSCC would take two photos of the same soil at the same time, which could later be used to create a 3-D image.

The image below was taken during Apollo 12. Find a pair of anaglyph glasses—paper "glasses" with a red filter on the left eye and a blue filter on the right. (You can make your own using colored cellophane and cardboard.) What do you see?

123RF.com, © pixelrobot

You can find other 3-D moon images online—just search using "ALSCC ana-glyph." You can also find other 3-D images created from other Apollo photos at www.lpi.usra.edu/resources/apollo/ or by searching on the term "Apollo anaglyph."

Courtesy of NASA/Lunar and Planetary Institute, AS12-57-8455

to Cone Crater. "We shouldn't have any trouble getting up there tomorrow," Mitchell reported to Houston. "There's certainly a lot of boulders on the side. I'd say some of them are 20 feet in diameter. . . . I think we can make it to the rim." For now, however, they needed to get some rest.

That was the plan. But midway through the night the astronauts were awakened by a loud bang.

"Did you hear that?" Shepard asked.

"I sure did," Mitchell said as they hopped out of their hammocks. They first worried that the lander might be tipping over—one of its pads had settled in a small crater, tilting the spacecraft. Or perhaps they'd been hit by a meteorite. They found nothing.

Neither man slept well that night.

Orbiting overhead in *Kitty Hawk*, Stu Roosa wasn't sleeping any better. He'd been assigned a long list of things to photograph, but the ship's camera was malfunctioning.

Occasionally, though, Roosa looked out the window at the view. Each time *Kitty Hawk* passed into the moon's shadow, a damp clamminess enveloped the capsule. It was like he could *feel* the moon's darkness. And then, when it burst back into sunlight, "you immediately start feeling better, just because there's sunlight coming through the windows," he recalled.

Early the next morning, Shepard and Mitchell left for Cone Crater, a mile to the east. The crater was almost 1,100 feet wide and 800 feet deep, and Mitchell had a map showing how to get there. It should have been easy to find, but it wasn't.

down in the lunar dust, and if a wheel hit a rock it would bounce up and nearly overturn.

Apollo 14's ALSEP was set up 650 feet from *Antares*. Mitchell then tested the ALSEP's seismometer using a "thumper." Thirteen times, at different locations, he fired explosive charges down into the lunar soil and the seismometer recorded the jolts. The data allowed geologists to better understand the moon's surface.

Four and a half hours later, the astronauts returned to *Antares*. The next day they would hike

One of the weird realities of the lunar surface was how difficult it was to judge distances, or to see features just yards away. Without the haze of an atmosphere, same-colored features blended together. Viewers who watched the first EVA on TV saw the astronauts mysteriously vanish down into the moonscape, then rise up on unseen hills as the pair walked into the distance.

Mitchell thought they were getting close to the crater's rim as they passed more boulders and the moondust got deeper. "You take two steps up, and you slip back one. It's like a day at the beach, plodding through deep sand," Shepard told Houston.

The pair struggled to drag the MET up the hill. Doctors monitoring their heart rates told them to take a moment to rest. Finally, they reached what they thought was the top of the rim, but it was just another small crater—the moonscape continued to rise even higher on the other side.

The CapCom relayed new instructions: "The word from the back room is they'd like you to consider where you are as the edge of Cone Crater."

Mitchell was frustrated. "I think you're finks," he replied.

The astronauts gave it one last push until Houston told them to stop. They gathered a few more samples, then started the long walk back to *Antares*. Later they'd learn they were 60 feet from the rim. "If we had thrown a rock we would have thrown it over the edge," said Mitchell.

After trudging back to *Antares*, Shepard had one last task, and it wasn't on the flight plan. "Houston . . . you might recognize what I have in my hand," he said to TV viewers, "the handle for the contingency sample. It just so happens to have a genuine 6-iron on the bottom of it."

With Deke Slayton's help, Shepard had smuggled the head of a 6-iron and two golf balls onto the lander. It attached to the crew's shovel handle.

"In my left hand I have a little white pellet that's familiar to millions of Americans. I'll drop it down," he continued. "I'm going to try a little sand-trap shot here."

The bulky moon suit prevented Shepard from using both hands, so he swung the club with one,

Ed Mitchell looks at a map as he and Shepard search for Cone Crater, February 6, 1971. *Courtesy of NASA, AS14-64-9089*

Moon Trees

Long before he was an astronaut, Stu Roosa was a smoke jumper for the US Forest Service. In the 1950s he parachuted into active wildfires in California and Oregon. Smoke jumper teams prevent fires from spreading by being the first to reach rugged mountain locations.

Because he loved trees, Roosa carried 500 seeds to the moon and back—five species: redwood, sweet gum, Douglas fir, loblolly pine, and sycamore. After the mission, the seeds were germinated, and the saplings were planted all over the globe. Some of these "moon trees" are in famous locations, like the White House, but others not, like an elementary school in Dillsburg, Pennsylvania. There is even a moon tree at Arlington National Cemetery outside Washington, DC. It was planted in 2005 by the Roosa family to honor their father, Stu, who died in 1994 and was buried at Arlington.

In this activity, find the moon tree that is closest to you. A list of trees can be found at https://en.wikipedia.org/wiki/Moon_tree. Plan a visit to the tree. How large has it grown since the 1970s?

In the fall, you may be able to find a seed or cone on the ground to grow a second-generation moon tree for your home or school.

digging out a small hole as the ball rolled away. "I got more dirt than ball," he said. He struck the second ball cleanly. "Miles and miles and miles!" (It actually went about 200 yards.)

Mitchell then got into the act. He grabbed a rod from the solar wind collector and tossed it like an Olympian. "There's the greatest javelin throw of the century," he pronounced.

Mitchell crawled back into *Antares* first. As he followed him in, hanging on the ladder, Shepard leaned back to get one more view of the crescent Earth. *What a beauty*, he thought. *What a beauty*.

Sailing Home

Antares left the moon in the evening, February 6, and rendezvoused with *Kitty Hawk* later that night. This time, the docking mechanism worked perfectly. Alan Shepard floated up to the hatch separating the two spacecraft and knocked.

"Who's there?" asked Roosa from the other side.

With the rocks and film transferred, *Kitty Hawk* undocked from the ascent module and headed back to Earth. On the three-day return trip, Mitchell spent time looking out the window and thinking about what he had just experienced. "I had a ringside seat to one of the greatest shows in the universe," he later wrote.

And then, out of the blue, a powerful feeling washed over him: he suddenly felt at one with the universe, that he finally understood how it all fit together. It surprised him and made him feel happy.

Apollo 14 splashed down in the Pacific Ocean near American Samoa on February 9. The crew were placed in an MQF on the USS *New Orleans* and transported back to Houston.

Midway through their 21-day quarantine, news leaked about a strange experiment that had taken place during the mission . . . and neither Shepard nor Roosa knew anything about it. On four different occasions, twice going to the moon and twice coming back, Ed Mitchell had been part of an ESP experiment.

ESP, the popular term for "extrasensory perception," is the belief that humans can communicate through thought alone. During four in-flight rest periods, Mitchell would write down, then stare at, a series of numbers that matched five different shapes. Back on Earth, four people tried to "perceive" which shapes Mitchell was "transmitting," then write them down.

There was only one problem—the launch of Apollo 14 was delayed 40 minutes, and the four people on Earth forgot to adjust their schedules. In other words, they were trying to receive Mitchell's messages via ESP 40 minutes *before* he even thought of them. Nevertheless, Mitchell claimed the experiment had worked.

None of this impressed the scientists working with NASA. Privately, many were angry. Several of the rock and soil samples Shepard and Mitchell had collected were poorly documented—it wasn't clear where the pair had picked them up. And yet Shepard could find time for his golf stunt, and Mitchell his ESP "experiments"?

There were only three Apollo missions left and the scientists were going to make the most of them. Even if they had to step on a few astronauts' toes.

What Would You Weigh?

When the astronauts walked on the moon, they and their suits weighed about 360 pounds . . . if measured on Earth. *On the moon, however, they weighed only 60 pounds. The moon's gravity is only one-sixth of Earth's gravity because the moon is less massive than the Earth.*

What would you *weigh on the moon?*

YOU'LL NEED

- Bathroom scale
- Calculator
- Laundry basket or box
- Heavy objects (books, bottle of water, etc.)

1. Weigh yourself on a bathroom scale.
2. Divide your Earth weight by six to determine your moon weight.
3. Place a laundry basket or sturdy box on the laundry scale. Fill the basket with heavy items, like books, until you reach your calculated moon weight.
4. Try to lift the basket. Can you do it?

7

The Science Missions

In the final days before the launch of Apollo 16, astronaut Ken Mattingly would go out after dinner to look around Pad 39A. "We'd spent years learning about the spacecraft and didn't know anything about the rocket," he admitted. "It was kind of a cool thing that I just wanted to see."

One night he spotted a light coming from inside the Saturn V's instrument unit. It was a technician doing a few last-minute checks. Mattingly introduced himself and asked how it all worked. "He was thrilled to show me around," said Mattingly. *"Here's this thing and this thing,* and pointed out what the boxes were and what he was going to do that night."

Apollo 16 astronaut John Young gives a jumping salute, April 21, 1972. *Courtesy of NASA, AS16-113-18339*

Finally, the man opened up to Mattingly. "I can't imagine what it's going to be like for you," he said. "But I can tell you this: it won't fail because of what I do."

That's the spirit of Apollo, Mattingly thought. Everyone he worked with, from Kennedy Space Center to Houston to the thousands of private contractors across the nation, was dedicated to the program.

For many, their work was coming to an end. NASA laid off 1,300 employees as the last missions approached. More would lose their jobs after the final flight, Apollo 17. In the communities around Kennedy Space Center, families lost their homes, and many moved away. But for those who remained, the spirit of Apollo continued until the final splashdown.

A Focus on Geology

Throughout Apollo, astronauts received geology training. But the program's early missions were far more concerned about how to get to the moon, not on what they might find once they got there. As the missions focused more on science, so did the training.

Back in June 1965, NASA had selected six new astronauts. All were scientists: three physicists, two doctors, and one geologist, a man named Jack Schmitt. The astronauts who'd come to NASA through the military took a while to warm up to them.

In time, Schmitt would bridge the gap between the astronauts and NASA's scientists. Four geolo-

gists, Gordon Swann, Lee Silver, Bill Muehlberger, and Farouk El-Baz, would be essential to Apollo's success.

Swann, Silver, and Muehlberger trained crews on weeklong field trips to remote locations—Hawaiian volcanoes, Earth craters, Iceland. They even rode deep into the Grand Canyon on burros. When the astronauts got to the moon, the geologists didn't want them to grab the first rocks they saw, but to study the lunar surface and look for unique specimens that would reveal the moon's history.

Farouk El-Baz trained the command module pilots. Since these crew members never went to the surface, they learned to study the moon's geology from orbit. The Egyptian-born geologist would fly with the CM pilots over mountains and deserts of the West to teach them how to identify rock formations from several miles up. He also helped Apollo planners select landing sites that promised the most interesting finds.

Apollo 15

On July 12, 1771, Captain James Cook sailed into the port at Deal, England, at the end of a three-year, round-the-world scientific expedition aboard the HMS *Endeavour*. Two hundred years later, Farouk El-Baz suggested the Apollo 15 crew name their CM *Endeavour*. For the LM they chose *Falcon*, the mascot for the US Air Force Academy. (All three astronauts served in the air force.)

Apollo 15 would spend two weeks in space, including nearly three days on the surface, where they would use a new lunar rover to drive miles from the lander. The mission would also orbit the moon for more than six days, photographing and studying the moon's surface.

On July 26, 1971, the launch date arrived. After a quick medical exam and breakfast, the crew suited up and headed out for Pad 39A. "When [the technicians] closed the hatch, it kinda clanged like a dungeon door," Irwin recalled. "I think that is when the reality of the situation hit me: I realized I was cut off from the world."

Apollo 15 lifted off in perfect weather at 9:34 AM. In Washington, President Nixon didn't bother getting out of bed to see it, though the White House told the press "he had watched it with great interest."

The three-day flight out was mostly trouble free. The command module sprang a leak in a water line. The crew patched it and cleaned up the mess. "We've got a bunch of towels hanging up," Scott reported. "Looks like somebody's laundry."

Apollo 15 reached the moon on July 29. The crew fired the CSM's engine on the far side and they entered orbit. "Hello Houston," Scott radioed as they came back into contact with Mission Control. "The *Endeavour*'s on destination with cargo, and what a fantastic sight."

A Tricky Landing

To get to its landing site, Apollo 15 would have to fly over the moon's Apennine Mountains, down through a valley with 15,000-foot peaks on both

The Apollo 15 crew (l to r): Dave Scott, Al Worden, and Jim Irwin. *Courtesy of NASA, S71-37963*

sides, and set down just short of a twisting, boulder-filled gorge called Hadley Rille.

Most of *Falcon*'s approach was controlled by computer. Scott and Irwin wouldn't get a good view of the landing site until the last few minutes before touchdown. As the LM descended, flying along on its back, the astronauts could only look up through its windows. What they saw shocked them: mountains. *Above* them.

Finally, *Falcon* rotated upright and Scott saw his destination. As he guided the lander in, 60 feet up, dust started to billow up and he couldn't see the surface. When the CONTACT light flashed, he cut off the engine and the *Falcon* dropped the last few feet with a crunch.

THE LUNAR ROVING VEHICLE

Apollo planners realized early on that if they wanted the astronauts to explore beyond walking distance from the lander, they'd need a vehicle. Three months before Apollo 11, they started designing a lunar roving vehicle (LRV). Seventeen months later, it was ready to go.

The battery-powered LRV folded up into a square shape that was 5 feet across and 20 inches thick. It was attached to the side of the LM "like a piano tied to a moving van," said astronaut Gene Cernan. Once lowered to the ground, the 460-pound rover could be unfolded and ready to go in 13 minutes.

The tires on the LRV were wire mesh, not rubber. Each wheel was powered by a motor about as powerful as an electric drill. The driver controlled the speed and direction with a T-bar controller between the two seats. A video camera was mounted on the front of the rover, which transmitted its signal to Earth through an umbrella-shaped TV antenna. The camera was controlled from Houston by an engineer named Ed Fendell, whom everyone called "Captain Video." The LRV also had its own navigation and communication systems to find its way around the moonscape. Rocks and equipment were stored in the rear.

Astronauts never drove the rover any farther than six miles from the lander, in case it broke down and they had to walk back. It never did. During Apollo 16, John Young set a speed record in the LRV—11 mph.

Courtesy of NASA, S71-00166

"Bam!" Irwin shouted.

Scott radioed Mission Control, "OK, Houston. The *Falcon* is on the plain at Hadley."

One of the lander's pads sank into a small crater, causing the LM to lean, lifting another pad off the ground. Beneath them, the engine bell had struck the crater's rim and bent.

Though they wouldn't leave *Falcon* for several more hours, Dave Scott took a look around. He opened the top docking hatch, climbed up on the ascent engine, and popped his head out of the lander. To the south, Mount Hadley rose three miles high, taller than any peak in the Rocky Mountains.

"Oh, boy, what a view!" he said. "All of the features around here are very smooth. The tops of the mountains are rounded off. There are no sharp, jagged peaks or no large boulders apparent anywhere." Scott went on for a half hour, but eventually closed the hatch. "There's just so much out there. I could talk to you for hours."

The two ate dinner, hung up their hammocks, and got five hours of rest. Irwin said it was the best sleep he'd had in three days.

On July 31, Scott descended from *Falcon* onto the moonscape. "As I stand out here in the wonders of the unknown at Hadley, I sort of realize there's a fundamental truth to our nature: man *must* explore. And this is exploration at its greatest."

This time the crew wouldn't be dragging a lunar rickshaw through the dust. Tucked into *Falcon*'s descent stage was a hi-tech moon buggy—the lunar roving vehicle.

Rocking and Rolling

Dave Scott yanked on a cord and the side of *Falcon* opened. The lunar rover dropped to the ground and unfolded like an origami car. While Irwin practiced walking in the one-sixth gravity, Scott jumped in the LRV and drove it in a circle around the lander.

After loading up the rover with gear, the pair buckled up—a must—and drove off on their first EVA.

"Man, this is really a rocking, rolling ride, isn't it?" Scott said.

Irwin agreed. "Never been on a ride like this before."

"Boy, oh boy!" cried Scott as they raced away at 7 mph.

The astronauts stopped occasionally to collect samples. Soon they were heading up Hadley Delta toward St. George Crater, a gigantic hole near the base of the mountain. They parked short of the crater and looked back toward *Falcon* and Hadley Rille, the deep gorge snaking across the plain.

"This is *spectacular!*" Scott exclaimed. "The most beautiful thing I've ever seen."

The astronauts photographed and collected samples at several more stops. They ended the EVA by setting up the mission's ALSEP. Scott had difficulty drilling a 10-foot core sample, and had to leave the jammed drill sticking out of the ground.

After reentering *Falcon* the two discovered another water leak. Almost three gallons had spilled on the floor around the ascent engine and

Astronaut Jim Irwin loads up the LRV for the first Apollo 15 EVA, July 31, 1971. Notice that *Falcon* is tilting backward. *Courtesy of NASA, AS15-86-11601*

all its electronics. They did their best to clean it up before eating and resting for the night.

On the second EVA, the pair returned to Hadley Delta. This time they drove three miles from the LM, rising 300 feet above the spacecraft on the plain below. Along the way, at Spur Crater, they discovered a boulder that was splattered with green glass. Irwin knocked off a piece with his hammer.

A half hour later, Irwin spotted another strange rock, about the size of a fist, perched atop a column of soil. It was white and had large crystals in it.

"Guess what we just found!" Scott laughed. "I think we found what we came for!"

It was a 4.1-billion-year-old hunk of anorthosite, part of the moon's original crust. It was a

Lunar sample #15415, the Genesis Rock. *Courtesy of NASA, S71-42951*

remarkable find, considering our solar system is only 4.6 billion years old. The press called it the "Genesis Rock."

On the way back to *Falcon*, Scott tried to remove the core sample drill again. No luck.

"Hello, Earth!"

"¡Hola, Tierra—saludos desde *Endeavor!*"

"Marhaba ahle el-ard—min *Endeavour* elaykum salaam!"

Each time Al Worden emerged from behind the moon in the CSM, he said the same thing: "Hello, Earth—greetings from *Endeavour!*" But each time he did, he used a different language.

"Gutten Tag, Erde—Grüße von *Endeavour!*"

Worden wanted to share this voyage with everyone. Before launch, he had gone on *Mister Rogers' Neighborhood* to explain the life of an astronaut. Now that he was orbiting the moon, he couldn't sleep—he was too excited.

"Shalom, aretz—B'ruchoth m'*Endeavour!*"

Worden had a lot of work to do. He used a mass spectrometer to see if the moon had a thin atmosphere. (It does, but just barely.) He used a radiation detector to find alpha particles produced by volcanic activity. And he took more than a mile of high-resolution film of the surface.

Down below, Dave Scott and Jim Irwin were starting their third and final EVA. After loading the LRV, the astronauts tried one more time to remove the core sample. This time it worked. Pulling together they yanked out the tube and eight and a half feet of lunar soil. Geologists would find 58 distinct layers in the sample, including particles emitted by the sun.

Next, they drove to Hadley Rille. As they approached, they could see different layers of soil on the opposite side of the three-quarter-mile-wide valley. They parked near the rille to collect rock samples, while the LRV's camera followed their movements.

"Out of sheer curiosity, how far back from . . . the edge of the rille are the two of you standing now?" CapCom Joe Allen asked, worried they were dangerously close to the 1,000-foot dropoff. "It looks like you are standing on the edge of a precipice." In actuality, the edge was a gentle slope.

Returning to *Endeavour*, Dave Scott mailed a letter. "I'm very proud to have the opportunity

Dave Scott and the LRV, with Hadley Rille behind, July 31, 1971.
Courtesy of NASA, AS15-85-11451

here to play postman," he said, canceling the envelope's stamp. "What could be a better place to cancel a stamp than right here at Hadley Rille?"

And then Scott performed one last experiment for TV viewers. It had been done originally in the late 1590s in Italy. "In my left hand I have a feather. In my right hand a hammer," Scott began. "I guess one of the reasons we got here today was because of a gentleman named Galileo, a long time ago, who made a rather significant discovery about falling objects in gravity fields. And we thought, where would be a better place to confirm his findings than on the moon? And so we thought we'd try it here for you, and the feather happens to be, appropriately, a falcon feather."

The feather came from the mascot of the US Air Force Academy, a trained falcon named Baggin. In his other hand Scott held a geology hammer. "I'll drop the two of them here and, hopefully, they'll hit the ground at the same time." Without an atmosphere to slow the feather, both fell at the same speed. "How about that!" he said. "Mr. Galileo was correct in his findings."

Scott then hopped in the rover and drove it to a hill 300 feet away, so that its camera could film *Falcon* taking off later that day. After parking, he placed a three-and-a-half-inch-tall statue of an aluminum man and a card listing the names of 14 men, both American and Soviet, who lost their lives in the space race. The sculpture by Belgian artist Paul van Hoeydonck was called *Fallen Astronaut*. Most of Mission Control had no idea Scott had brought it along, nor did they know he had left it until they saw the photo he'd taken.

While Scott parked the rover, Irwin found himself with 15 free minutes. "I just figured it was my time to relax, so I just ran around the lunar module a few times, and I tried to do leaps across craters. And just felt like a little kid at recess time."

With 170 pounds of rocks and samples loaded into the LM, the astronauts tossed out everything they could to lighten the spacecraft—their backpacks, empty food containers, and bags of human waste. At 12:11 PM (Houston time), *Falcon* took off. The crew rendezvoused two hours later. After transferring the rocks, experiments, cameras, and film, they grabbed a few souvenirs from *Falcon*— utility lights and other loose parts. But in their

Fallen Astronaut on the moon, August 2, 1971. On the card: Ted Freeman, Charlie Bassett, Elliot See, Gus Grissom, Roger Chaffee, Ed White, Vladimir Komarov, Ed Givens, C. C. Williams, Yuri Gagarin, Pavel Belyayev, Georgy Dobrovolsky, Viktor Patsayev, and Vladislav Volkov. *Courtesy of NASA, AS15-11894*

Feather Drop

In this activity, recreate Galileo's experiment with a heavy object and a light object, though not a feather, as Dave Scott did—you're not in a vacuum, after all.

YOU'LL NEED

- Heavy object (like a baseball—nothing breakable)
- Light object (like a small screw)

1. Find a safe location for the experiment—a second-story window or balcony overlooking a lawn or sidewalk.
2. Compare two objects—one heavy and one light. Do you think one will fall faster than the other?
3. Making sure nobody is below, release the objects at the same time and watch them drop.
4. Which hit the ground first? Try this experiment several times to see if the results are the same.

Bonus: Search YouTube for the video of Scott's hammer-and-feather experiment.

rush, they missed transferring a few PPKs. Wedding rings, medallions, flags, and a packet of $2 bills—all were lost forever when the ascent module undocked and crashed back into the moon.

Celebration and Scandal

Apollo 15 orbited for another two days taking photos and launching a small satellite that would circle the moon for the next year, studying the moon's magnetic field.

On August 4, they were ready to head back. "Set your sails for home. We're predicting good weather, a strong tailwind, and we'll be waiting on the dock," said CapCom Allen, giving the crew the go-ahead for transearth injection.

While returning, Al Worden performed the first-ever deep-space EVA to retrieve cameras and experiments mounted outside the CSM. "When we opened the hatch it was just like a vacuum cleaner pulling all the loose stuff from the inside out into space," Irwin wrote. "Everything started floating out. My toothbrush floated by; it had been hiding. A camera came by; one of us grabbed it. We were all leaping around, trying to catch the important stuff." Fortunately, they didn't lose anything valuable.

Though they didn't know it at the time, the crew also made a remarkable discovery. On the way back they did an x-ray scan of deep space. Astronomers later found a "hole" in the scan where no x-rays existed, almost as if they'd been swallowed up. And they had—it was the first proof that black holes exist.

On August 7 the astronauts were awakened by the "Hawaiian War Chant," piped over the radio. The USS *Okinawa* was waiting to recover *Endeavour* 285 miles north of Oahu. When the CM finally broke through the clouds it narrowly missed hitting a recovery helicopter. Only two of its three parachutes were inflated, and the capsule was coming down fast. Worden had dumped all the remaining thruster fuel while descending, and it had blown up into the nylon cords and dissolved one set. Another chute was starting to fail when the capsule hit the ocean. Dave Scott, who had flown on Apollo 9, thought the impact was twice as hard as he'd felt before. But they were home.

On this flight, NASA had eliminated the quarantine, so the crew was able to leave the capsule without protective suits or respirators. "I get into the raft and, man, it's great. Beautiful. Nice and warm," Irwin recalled. "The first thing I do is dip my hand in the ocean and put the water on my face. Just to feel that water—water from the earth on your face—and to feel that air."

Apollo 15 was considered a milestone in US spaceflight, and a huge step forward in space science. But within a year, the mission was mired in scandal.

Before the flight, a German stamp collector had approached Dave Scott with an offer: he would give Scott 400 stamped envelopes to bring along and cancel on the moon's surface, then autograph. Each astronaut would keep 100 envelopes and the dealer the last 100. He would also set up a $6,000 scholarship fund for each astronaut's family, for their children. None of the envelopes were to be sold until after the astronauts had left NASA. But the dealer began selling them immediately, and the press found out.

Scott, Worden, and Irwin were eventually dragged before the US Senate and questioned.

One parachute collapsed during Apollo 15's splashdown, August 7, 1971. *Courtesy of NASA, S71-41999*

They apologized, but their careers came to an end, all for doing something astronauts had done since Mercury, and likely still do today.

What should have been an even greater scandal, wasn't. During Jim Irwin's first lunar EVA, he became dehydrated and suffered a mild heart attack. Irwin was not told this had happened, and performed two more lunar EVAs, and the deep-space EVA with Worden. Had he suffered another heart attack, it could have jeopardized all the men's lives.

Apollo 16

When Apollo 16 astronaut Charlie Duke arrived at the launch tower, there was a sign inside the capsule. It read, Typhoid Mary's Seat, a reference

The Apollo 16 crew (l to r): Ken Mattingly, John Young, and Charlie Duke. *Courtesy of NASA, S72-16660*

volcanic activity. The astronauts would also use a lunar rover to explore the craters and hills surrounding the landing site.

As the launch clock counted down, Duke said Young was calm—this was his fourth spaceflight, after all—while Mattingly "was as keyed up as I and was intently watching the instrument panel in front of him." When the Saturn V roared into the sky at 12:54 PM, Young's heartbeat barely increased. Duke's doubled.

Later, as the astronauts prepared for their first night's sleep, Duke opened his flight plan and found two crayon drawings from his sons. The oldest, Charles, wrote, "We love you," and Tom wished him, "Have a safe trip home." He also found a card from his wife, Dotty. "When you look out at the moon and stars, remember we are looking at the same moon and stars and are close to you," she wrote.

The three-day translunar coast was uneventful, though Ken Mattingly somehow lost his wedding ring during a bathroom break. Also, the astronauts kept hearing a mysterious man on the radio, speaking in Spanish to his love interest. Nobody could figure out where it was coming from.

Apollo 16 entered lunar orbit on April 19. The following day, *Casper* and *Orion* undocked for Young and Duke to land. The two spacecraft were cruising around the far side of the moon, not far apart, when Mattingly noticed something wrong with the CSM. *Orion* was just minutes from firing its descent engine when Mattingly told Young to stop.

Mattingly had been testing the CSM's engine system when the spaceship began shaking. If

to an Irish American woman who unknowingly spread typhoid fever in New York during the early 1900s. Back on Apollo 13, it was Duke who had contracted German measles and exposed Ken Mattingly to the disease, bumping Mattingly from the flight.

The whole crew laughed, especially Mattingly, who ended up as Apollo 16's CM pilot alongside Duke. John Young was the commander. The astronauts named their CM *Casper* (they thought the moon suits made them look like cartoon ghosts) and the LM *Orion*, for the hunter constellation.

Apollo 16 was headed for the Descartes Highlands, where geologists hoped to find evidence of something was seriously wrong with the CSM's engine, the crew would need the LM's descent engine to get home.

Mission Control told the crew to stay in orbit while they investigated the problem. "Anticipate a wave-off for this one," the CapCom said, which was NASA-speak for "This mission could be scrubbed."

"Our hearts sank," recalled Duke. "There we were, two years of training, 240,000 miles away, an hour before the landing . . . and they're about to tell you to come home."

Orion orbited the moon with *Casper* for the next six hours. NASA ran simulations to determine what was happening, and whether it posed a danger. When Apollo 16 emerged from the far side on its 15th orbit, Mission Control had decided: "You do have a Go for another try here at PDI," the CapCom said. They were cleared for landing.

"Piece of Cake"

As with earlier missions, Apollo 16 kicked up dust. "When we leveled off at 20 feet, I remember looking out . . . you really couldn't see through the dust that was being blasted away," Duke recalled. But Young ignored the dust; he was watching *Orion's* shadow. As he neared the shadow, he knew he was close to the surface.

"Contact!" Duke shouted.

Young counted *one-potato* in his head, then shut off the engine, dropping the last three feet.

The astronauts quickly checked the lander, then Young looked out the window. "Well, we don't have to walk far to pick up rocks, Houston," he said, almost ho-hum. And the landing? "Piece of cake."

Duke was the opposite—he couldn't contain himself. "Fantastic!! Percy Precision [his nickname for Young] has planted one on the Plains of Descartes!" Judging from the craters outside, Duke could tell they were just a few yards off their landing target.

SPACE WASTE

It's the question astronauts get more than any other: *How do you go to the bathroom in space?*

It isn't easy. To poop during Apollo an astronaut would use a plastic bag with an adhesive strip around the opening. He would remove his space suit, attach the bag to his buttocks, and then defecate. But without gravity, the waste wouldn't drop down or away. "You are floating, the bag is floating, and everything else is floating!" Charlie Duke recalled. After pushing the waste down into the bag, the astronaut would add a germicide to the bag, knead it together, and store it for doctors to study later.

Urinating was a little easier. The astronaut would use a hose that was connected to the outside. Turning a valve on the hose would create suction and pull the urine out into space. "It was an incredibly beautiful sight as the urine hit the vacuum outside, crystallizing into very fine droplets and creating a mist of millions of tiny rainbows," Duke remembered. "For a few minutes our spacecraft would be surrounded by these colorful rainbows, until the prisms of ice crystals floated off into space and disappeared."

It had been a long day. Mission Control told them to finish their checklists, eat, and rest up. The following morning, John Young crawled out of *Orion* and descended the ladder. "There you are, mysterious and unknown Descartes highland plains. Apollo 16 is gonna change your image," he said as he stepped onto the soil.

Duke didn't wait. "Here I come, babe!" he said, then wiggled through the hatch and hopped on the ladder. "Hot dog!! Is this great!"

The pair quickly unfolded the lunar rover, loaded it up, and erected the flag. Duke walked away from the LM with the camera and asked

Young to give a jumping salute (see page 114). Mission Control came over the radio a minute later and told the astronauts that Congress had approved NASA's budget, which included money for a new program, the Space Shuttle.

Young and Duke began setting up the ALSEP. Each experiment was attached to a central station by a "spaghetti bowl full of cables," as Duke described it. One of those cables got tangled in Young's boot, and he accidentally ripped it out of the heat-flow experiment.

"I'm sorry," said Young, upset. "I didn't even know. . . . I didn't even know it. . . . Aggh—it's sure gone."

There was nothing to do but move on. The astronauts headed west in the LRV. They passed Plum Crater, Spook Crater, Flag Crater, and Buster Crater, collecting samples along the route, then turned around and traced their tracks back to *Orion* to end the day.

Deke Slayton, who had been denied his chance to go to space during Mercury, took over CapCom duty as the astronauts ate dinner and prepared to rest. "It sounds like the best place in the world to sleep. I wish I was with you," he said.

"We do, too, boss," Duke replied.

Stone Mountain and House Rock

The second EVA took the astronauts to the top of Stone Mountain, about four miles south. Duke was surprised how well the rover worked. "Going up Stone Mountain, it felt like we were going out

Charlie Duke at Plum Crater during Apollo 16's first EVA, April 21, 1972. *Courtesy of NASA, AS16-114-18423*

the back of the seat, because it was a pretty steep hill," he said.

At the top, they looked back across the valley floor 500 feet below, gouged by craters and littered with boulders. "It was awesome," Duke remembered. "There was a distinct gap between the lunar surface and the blackness of space, and the lunar module sitting in the middle of the valley. It was a dramatic moment. The emotion, the beauty of the moon."

After another rest period at *Orion*, the astronauts set out on their third and final EVA. This journey would take them to the North Ray Crater, which they had seen from Stone Mountain the day before.

North Ray was enormous, and deep. Young pulled up to the rim in the LRV. "Man, does that thing have steep walls," he said.

"They said sixty degrees," replied Duke.

"I tell you, I can't see to the bottom of it, and I'm just as close to the edge as I'm going to get," said Young.

The camera on the LRV made it appear that the astronauts were closer to the rim than they really were. Some in Mission Control were nervous they might tumble in. A ground controller panned the camera back and forth, and geologists noticed a large boulder in the distance. They asked the astronauts to get a sample.

Again, distances were deceiving. "We kept jogging and jogging, and the rock kept getting bigger and bigger and bigger," recalled Duke. And on camera, the men got smaller and smaller. "We didn't sense [it] at first, and so we get down to this

thing and we called it 'House Rock.' You know, it must've been 90 feet across and 45 feet tall. It was humongous."

Young used his hammer to knock off a chunk. Later, back on Earth, geologists would use it to prove the moon's surface had not formed volcanically, as Earth's had.

After returning to *Orion*, Young and Duke began packing up. Duke took a moment to step away from the lander, where he pulled a plastic-wrapped photo out of his pocket. It was a picture of his family—he and Dotty and their sons Charlie, 7, and Tom, 5. On the back he had written, "This is the family of Astronaut Duke from Planet Earth. Landed on the Moon, April 1972." All four had autographed it. Duke placed the photo on the lunar soil and returned to the LM.

The astronauts had been planning a stunt—the Moon Olympics—but they were running out of time. Still, Duke tried to show just how high he could jump, hopping up and down several times until he tipped over backward.

"I was in trouble. You could watch me scrambling like that, trying to get my balance. I ended up landing on my right side, and bouncing on to my back. And my heart was just pounding," said Duke. "If my spacesuit splits, I'm dead."

Young rushed over to help Duke up. "Charlie, that ain't very smart."

"That ain't very smart," Duke sheepishly agreed. "Well, I'm sorry about that."

Orion left the moon 71 hours after it landed. After docking with *Casper*, the crew orbited the moon for another day. The mission plan called for

The Duke family photo on the moon, April 23, 1972. *Courtesy of NASA, AS16-117-18841*

Orion's ascent module blasting off, photographed by the LRV's TV camera, April 23, 1972. *Courtesy of NASA, S72-35613*

thousands of photos, experiments, and 213 pounds of rock and soil samples.

It was another impressive Apollo flight. Yet few Americans were even watching. *Life* magazine, which had chronicled the space race from the beginning, didn't even run a story on the mission. Instead, it printed just two Apollo 16 photos alongside a shot of First Lady Pat Nixon in a pioneer bonnet using a washboard at a North Carolina folk festival.

Apollo 17, the End of the Beginning

Apollo 17 would be the final moon mission, and commander Gene Cernan wanted people to remember it. In the months before launch, Cernan hounded the press. Interviews, photos, private tours—Cernan gave them whatever they wanted. This would be the best flight yet, he promised. "Apollo 17 may be the last flight to the moon, but it's not the end," he said. "It's the end of the beginning."

This final mission saw the first geologist/astronaut on its crew, LM pilot Jack Schmitt. "Dr. Rock," as many called him, was one of the few people allowed to experiment on lunar samples from earlier missions. At one time, Schmitt suggested Apollo 17 should try to land on the far side of the moon and communicate with Houston through a satellite placed in lunar orbit. The idea was expensive and dangerous. NASA planners finally had to ask him to stop bugging them—it wasn't going to happen.

a two-day orbit, but they left early because they were concerned about the SPS engine. "The more you waited up there—if you did have a problem—the less time you had to think of something brilliant to fix it," explained Duke.

On the flight back, Ken Mattingly performed an EVA to gather film from the service module's cameras. After crawling out the hatch, Charlie Duke stood up behind him to help. Duke then saw something shiny float out of the hatch and bounce off Mattingly's helmet. It was the wedding ring he had lost earlier! Duke snatched it, and when Mattingly returned to the capsule Duke said calmly, "Ken, I've got something for you."

Casper returned to Earth on April 27, 1972. It splashed down in the central Pacific a mile from the USS *Ticonderoga*. They brought with them

Ron Evans was named CM pilot. The Vietnam veteran was called "Captain America" around NASA because of his enthusiastic patriotism, even by astronaut standards. It was little surprise that the crew named the CM *America*. The LM was called *Challenger*, after a 19th-century research ship, the HMS *Challenger*.

Several weeks before Apollo 17 was scheduled to launch, NASA learned that Black September, a terrorist group that had murdered 11 Israeli athletes at the 1972 Munich Olympics, was now threatening to attack the astronauts' families while the crew was headed to the moon. The story was never reported at the time, but the astronauts' wives and children were given round-the-clock security until the mission was over.

Night Launch

More than a million spectators came to watch the final Apollo launch. Though scheduled to lift off the evening of December 6, 1972, it was delayed several hours for technical problems, then blasted off at 12:33 AM on December 7.

"It's lighting up the sky! It's just like daylight here at Kennedy Space Center!" shouted the flight announcer. The astronauts' families watched the Saturn V from a spot near the Banana River. The bright orange flame and deafening roar scared the fish, which jumped out of the water. The glow from the launch could be seen from as far away as North Carolina.

Apollo 17 had no problems on its three-day flight to the moon. Cernan's only complaint was

The Apollo 17 crew: (standing, l to r) Jack Schmitt and Ron Evans, (seated) Gene Cernan.
Courtesy of NASA, S72-50438

that Jack Schmitt, always the observant scientist, just wouldn't shut up. He described land formations and weather patterns back on Earth, even reporting, "Hey, there's Antarctica. It's all full of snow!" When Earth became too small to see in detail, he jabbered on about the rapidly approaching moon.

America entered lunar orbit on December 10. *Columbia* was scheduled to descend to the surface the next day. It would be tricky, Cernan admitted. "[The] valley where we were to land in was surrounded by mountains on three sides that are higher than the Grand Canyon is deep," he

Cernan turned to Schmitt. "Boy, when you said shut down, I shut down and we dropped, didn't we?"

"Yes, sir! But we is here," said Schmitt.

Cernan smiled. "Man, is we here."

In the Valley of Taurus-Littrow

When Gene Cernan stepped off *Challenger* four hours after landing, he said, "Houston, as I step off at the surface at Taurus-Littrow, we'd like to dedicate the first step of Apollo 17 to all those who made it possible."

Schmitt followed a few minutes later. Surveying the hills and craters that surrounded them, he said, "A geologist's paradise, if I ever saw one."

Soon, awe gave way to excitement. "Oh, bury me not on the lone prairie! Where the coyotes howl, and the wind blows free!" Dr. Rock sang, while digging through the rover for the flag they'd brought. It wasn't just any American flag; this flag had been carried to the moon on Apollo 11, and had hung in Mission Control ever since. Now it would mark Apollo's final trip to the moon.

After planting the flag, the astronaut set up the ALSEP. Cernan accidentally whacked the rover with his rock hammer, breaking off its right rear fender. When they started driving, the wheel kicked up the lunar soil and showered it down on them.

The first EVA took the pair to Steno Crater, a short drive south of the lander. Cernan sang along with Schmitt as they hopped across the moonscape, looking for specimens.

explained. "So at 7,000 feet we were down among them. I mean the mountains rose above us on both sides." North Massif was on their right, South Massif on their left, and Family Mountain was three miles away, dead ahead.

As they descended, Cernan took control from the computer. "Long before that, I told Jack, I said, 'Jack, don't talk to me, I don't need the information you're giving me.' I know he kept calling the fuel out and one thing or another. By that time I didn't need to hear anything else."

At 1:54 PM in Houston, *Challenger* dropped the final few feet to the surface. For the first time on the mission, Schmitt was speechless.

"OK, Houston, the *Challenger* has landed," radioed Cernan, and the CapCom sent congratulations.

After seven hours outside, the astronauts returned to *Challenger* to eat and rest. But Cernan didn't want to sleep. "Who wants to go to the moon to sleep? That's when you have a chance to think about these things. Think about what you just saw and where you are."

The next morning, the astronauts repaired the LRV's fender using four lunar maps, screw clamps, and duct tape. They then headed out for the South Massif, an imposing mountain five miles to the southwest, then back along an area called Tortilla Flat. Along the way they stopped at Shorty Crater where Schmitt made an important discovery, entirely by accident.

Cernan had walked off to take photos, and Schmitt was looking for interesting rocks. Then he noticed something strange about his footprints in the dust.

"Oh, hey!" Schmitt called out. "There is *orange* soil!"

Cernan didn't sound impressed. "Well, don't move it until I see it."

"It's all over! Orange!!" Schmitt went on.

"Don't move it till I see it," Cernan repeated.

"I stirred it up with my feet."

Cernan finally saw what Schmitt found. "Hey, it is! I can see it from here!"

"It's orange!" Schmitt shouted.

Both astronauts understood that orange soil could be the volcanic evidence they were searching for. Perhaps Shorty wasn't a crater, but a volcanic vent. Cernan pounded a three-foot tube into the soil for a core sample. When it was analyzed later on Earth, it was discovered to have come

THE BLUE MARBLE

On December 7, 1972, astronaut Jack Schmitt took a color photo of Earth through the window of the Apollo 17 command module. Taken 34,000 miles out, it showed the continent of Africa, the Arabian Peninsula, and Antarctica. And because the planet appeared so complete, so round, the photo became known as *The Blue Marble*, or sometimes *Whole Earth*.

Nobody had seen anything quite like it, except a few lucky astronauts. "You look back at the earth, which is surrounded by the blackest black you can imagine, and you get a sense of the endlessness of time and space," Gene Cernan said. "It's overwhelming, unrealistic. You grasp for your identity at that moment. You just want to have everyone standing next to you, feeling what you feel."

Today, there are few people who have *not* seen it. *The Blue Marble* is believed to be the most reproduced photo in human history.

Courtesy of NASA, AS17-148-22727

Making Craters

By studying the moon, scientists could determine what meteorites hit the lunar surface by the size of the craters they made. So can you!

YOU'LL NEED

- White flour
- Powdered cocoa
- Sifter
- Pie tin
- Marbles or stones (small and large)

1. Fill a metal pie tin with flour and level it out.
2. Using a sifter, sprinkle powdered cocoa over the flour until it is mostly covered.
3. This will be messy. Move outside, or to a garage.
4. Drop different marbles into the pie tin from at least a foot above.
5. Compare the craters made in the flour and cocoa. How are they shaped? Do they have rims? Where does the splattered material go?

Bonus: Compare your craters to photos of moon craters in this book: pages 61, 70, and 91. Do they look similar?

Orange soil at Shorty Crater, December 12, 1972. *Courtesy of NASA, AS17-137-20990*

from a "fire fountain," a gassy eruption from a lava flow 3.7 billion years earlier. Shorty *was* an impact crater, one that had pushed up the orange soil to the surface.

The astronauts made a third rover trip the next day, this time toward the North Massif. As he had on earlier drives, Schmitt placed explosive grenades along the route that were detonated later by Mission Control to test the moon's crust.

In three rover EVAs, the crew had driven 19 miles and collected 243 pounds of rocks. One of the last rocks was chosen specifically to be given away—the Goodwill Moon Rock.

"It's a rock composed of many fragments, of many sizes, and many shapes," Cernan explained to TV viewers. "When we return this rock, or some of the others like it to Houston, we'd like to share a piece of this rock with so many of the countries throughout the world. We hope that this will be a symbol of what our feelings are, what the feelings of the Apollo program are, and a symbol of mankind: that we can live in peace and harmony in the future." Back on Earth, it was broken into small pieces that were presented to 135 different world leaders and 50 US governors.

Finally, Cernan drove the rover off into the distance and parked it to face *Challenger*. Before walking back, he leaned over and wrote his daughter Tracy's initials, T D C, in the dust using his gloved finger.

And then it was time to leave. Before climbing the ladder, Cernan remarked, "As we leave the moon at Taurus-Littrow, we leave as we came, and, God willing, as we shall return, with peace and hope for all mankind. Godspeed the crew of Apollo 17."

The Final Trip Home

Challenger blasted off from the moon at 4:55 PM Houston time on December 14, 1972. It reunited with *America* two hours later. As the crew transferred their samples and equipment to the CM, Mission Control interrupted to read a message from the president.

"As the *Challenger* leaves the surface of the moon, we are conscious not of what we leave behind, but of what lies before us," it began, followed by Nixon's thoughts about the hopes of humanity. "This may be the last time in this century that men will walk on the moon, but space exploration will continue, the benefits of space exploration will continue, and there will be new dreams to pursue." The message continued, but Jack Schmitt had heard enough.

"I thought that was the stupidest thing a president ever could have said to anybody," he recalled, referring to the last-time-on-the-moon comment. "You may believe it privately, but why say it to the young people in the world. . . . It was just a totally unnecessary thing for him to say. Whoever wrote that speech really blew it with that remark. And I was really upset. Tired, but really mad. It was just pure loss of will."

Commander Gene Cernan (left) and Ron Evans, December 19, 1972. *Courtesy of NASA, AS17-162-24053*

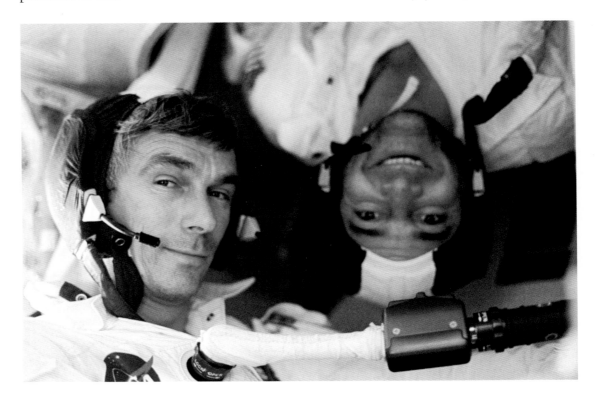

Apollo 17 orbited the moon for another two days. Five passengers—Fe, Fi, Fo, Fum, and Phooey—also rode along. They were mice sent to test the effects of cosmic radiation on living creatures. Four survived the voyage with no problems. (Why the fifth died was never determined.)

On the flight back, Ron Evans performed an EVA to remove film from the cameras on the service module. Because the space walk was being televised, Evans said hello to those back home.

"Hey, this is great! Talk about being a spaceman—this is it. . . . Hello mom!" he said, waving at the camera, then gave a shout out to his kids. "Hello, Jan. Hi, John—how are you doing? Hi, Jamie!" Evans was stalling, taking videos of the

moon and Earth, and the CapCom told him to come back in.

"I was having a ball," he admitted later. "You go outside, and you're hanging on, maneuvering out there from the safety and security of your mother ship. If you ever wanted to be a spaceman, that's the way to do it!"

Apollo 17 splashed down in the Pacific on December 19, 1972. The USS *Ticonderoga* waited three miles away. By coincidence, the *Ticonderoga* was the same aircraft carrier on which Ron Evans had been stationed during his service in Vietnam.

Standing on the deck of the *Ticonderoga*, Gene Ceran spoke to the sailors. "There's a fundamental law of nature, that either you must grow or you must die. Whether that be an idea, whether that be a man, whether that be a flower or a country. I thank God that our country has chosen to grow," he said.

Jan Evans met her husband when the crew returned to Houston. The family drove home together, where they were met by cheering neighbors. "Both sides of the street, all the way from the entrance into our cul-de-sac, was lined with flagpoles with the flag flying," she remembered. "There were people on horseback carrying flags, and any child that had a bicycle or tricycle had red, white, and blue decorated streamers and in their wheels and everything. Everybody felt a part of this program and a part of this community. They were proud."

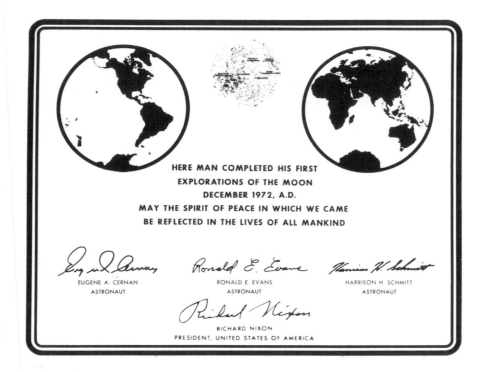

Courtesy of NASA, 72-H-1541

HERE MAN COMPLETED HIS FIRST
EXPLORATIONS OF THE MOON
DECEMBER 1972, A.D.
MAY THE SPIRIT OF PEACE IN WHICH WE CAME
BE REFLECTED IN THE LIVES OF ALL MANKIND

EUGENE A. CERNAN
ASTRONAUT

RONALD E. EVANS
ASTRONAUT

HARRISON H. SCHMITT
ASTRONAUT

RICHARD NIXON
PRESIDENT, UNITED STATES OF AMERICA

THE END OF APOLLO

Though the moon missions came to an end in 1972, NASA used the technology it developed for several more flights. When Apollo 20 was canceled, NASA found itself with a spare Saturn V. The rocket only needed its first two stages to get into Earth orbit, so a plan developed to convert its third stage into a space station, Skylab, which would orbit the Earth.

There were three missions to Skylab, each carrying three astronauts. The space station was launched without a crew on May 14, 1973. One minute after launch, its meteoroid shield rattled loose and damaged its solar panels. Without its protective shield and electrical supply, the laboratory appeared doomed.

Apollo 12's Pete Conrad commanded the Skylab rescue mission. The crew was able to shield the spacecraft and restore electrical power, and stayed aboard for 28 days. Alan Bean led the next flight, which lasted twice as long. The final mission lasted 84 days—almost three months. Then Skylab was abandoned. Earth's atmosphere finally dragged it down on July 11, 1979, after 3,896 orbits. Several large pieces crashed near the town of Esperance in Western Australia.

The last Apollo-related mission was a fitting end to the space race. Starting in late 1969, the Soviet Union and the United States began discussing how they might rescue the other country's astronauts/cosmonauts in an emergency. Talks became more serious following Apollo 13 and the deaths of three cosmonauts on Soyuz 11. The result was the Apollo-Soyuz Test Project (ASTP).

The goal of the ASTP was to demonstrate that spacecraft from the two countries could be made to rendezvous and dock in space. This would require not only a docking module to connect them, but cooperation on the part of both space agencies.

The Soviets selected two cosmonauts: Alexei Leonov, who was the first person to "walk" in space, and Valeri Kubasov. The Americans chose Tom Stafford to be commander, and two rookies to complete the crew: Vance Brand and 51-year-old Deke Slayton.

An artist's depiction of the Apollo and Soyuz spacecraft docking in orbit. *Courtesy of NASA, S74-24913*

Deke Slayton, ready for his first spaceflight. *Courtesy of NASA, S74-15240*

In a strange twist, Deke Slayton had unexpectedly cured his heart problem in 1970 when he took vitamins for a cold. Grounded since Mercury, he underwent extensive medical tests and was returned to the astronaut pool.

Both spacecraft launched on July 15, 1975. "I love it!" Slayton exclaimed as the Apollo capsule reached orbit. "Yowee! I've never felt so free!" Two days later, the spaceships docked and opened their hatches.

"Friend!" Stafford called out in Russian. "Come in here!"

"Very, very happy to see you. How are things?" Leonov replied in English.

The men exchanged gifts, ate meals together, and conducted experiments over the next two days. At one point, President Gerald Ford spoke with the crews.

"As the world's oldest space rookie, do you have any advice for young people who hope to fly on future space missions?" Ford asked Slayton.

"Never give up. Decide what you want to do and then never give up until you've done it," Slayton replied.

Most of the Apollo astronauts left NASA before the end of the 1970s, though John Young commanded the first Space Shuttle flight on April 12, 1981. Some took jobs in earthbound businesses, while others went into public service as ambassadors and elected officials. Mike Collins became the founding director of the Smithsonian Institution's National Air and Space Museum, which opened in 1976 for the nation's bicentennial.

Several astronauts found themselves changed by their experiences. Al Bean decided to pursue his passion for painting, becoming what he called an "explorer artist." Al Worden was drawn to poetry and published a collection of Apollo poems in 1974. Gene Cernan became a public speaker to promote the exploration of space. "I do know deep down in my heart that there is a young boy or a young girl out there . . . given the opportunity, an opportunity that has to be created by you and me, I do believe that they will one day take us back there," he said.

Jim Irwin's change was spiritual. He said he had felt the presence of God on the moon, and it deepened his Christian faith. He wrote, "Looking back at that spaceship we call earth, I was touched by a desire to convince man that he has a unique place to live, that he is a unique creature, and that he must learn to live with his neighbors."

Bill Anders, who had been a devout Catholic before Apollo 8, lost his faith. "When I looked back and saw that tiny Earth, it snapped my world view," he said. "Here we are, on kind of a physically inconsequential planet, going around a not particularly significant star, going around a galaxy of billions of stars that's not a particularly significant galaxy—in a universe where there's billions and billions of galaxies. Are we really that special? I don't think so."

Ed Mitchell, who conducted the ESP experiment on Apollo 14, devoted himself to the exploration of the mind, founding the Institute for Noetic Sciences in 1973. "I now felt a strong aversion to war and became a peacenik," he said. Rusty Schweickart became a follower of Zen Buddhism.

Many of the Apollo astronauts have passed away. At Johnson Space Center in Houston there is a living monument called the Astronaut Memorial Grove, one tree for each deceased astronaut. Each holiday season, the trees are wrapped in white lights to create a forest of stars. But one tree, the one honoring Apollo 12's Pete Conrad, is always decorated with red and green bulbs. Conrad, who years earlier yelled "Whoopie!" when he first stepped on the moon, had a personal motto: "If you can't be good, be colorful." Like so many of the Apollo astronauts, he was both.

GLOSSARY OF ACRONYMS

ALSCC Apollo Lunar Surface Closeup Camera

ALSEP Apollo Lunar Surface Experiments Package

AMU Astronaut Maneuvering Unit

ASTP Apollo-Soyuz Test Project

ATDA Augmented Target Docking Adaptor

BIG Biological Isolation Garment

CapCom Capsule Communicator

CM Command Module (capsule)

CSM Command and Service Module

EVA Extravehicular Activity (a space walk)

LCG Liquid Cooling Garment (first layer of moon suit)

LM Lunar Module (formerly LEM for Lunar Excursion Module)

LOC Launch Operations Center (later Kennedy Space Center)

LOI Lunar Orbit Insertion

LOX Liquid Oxygen

LRL Lunar Receiving Laboratory

LRV Lunar Roving Vehicle

MET Modular Equipment Transporter ("lunar rickshaw")

MQF Mobile Quarantine Facility

MSC Manned Spacecraft Center (later Johnson Space Center)

MSFC Marshall Space Flight Center

NACA National Advisory Council for Astronautics

NASA National Aeronautics and Space Administration

PDI Powered Descent Initiation

PLSS Portable Life-Support System (space suit backpack)

PPK Personal Preference Kit

SM Service Module (back end of the CSM)

SPS Service Propulsion System (engine)

TEI Transearth Injection

TLC Translunar Coast

TLI Translunar Injection

VAB Vertical (later Vehicle) Assembly Building

LEARN MORE ABOUT APOLLO

Books for Young Adults

Collins, Michael. *Flying to the Moon: An Astronaut's Journey.* Rev. ed. New York: Square Fish, 1994.

Dixon-Engel, Tara, and Mike Jackson. *Neil Armstrong: One Giant Leap for Mankind.* New York: Sterling, 2008.

Mitchell, Edgar. *Earthrise: My Adventures as an Apollo 14 Astronaut.* Chicago: Chicago Review Press, 2014.

Olson, Tod. *Lost in Outer Space: The Incredible Journey of Apollo 13.* New York: Scholastic, 2017.

Ottaviani, Jim, Zonder Cannon, and Kevin Cannon. *T-Minus: The Race to the Moon.* New York: Aladdin, 2009.

Shetterly, Margot Lee. *Hidden Figures: The American Dream and the Untold Story of the Black Women Mathematicians Who Helped Win the Space Race, Young Readers' Edition.* New York: William Morrow, 2016.

Films

NASA made short documentaries of all the Apollo missions, with fascinating footage from the flights. Today you can find them on YouTube.

Apollo 4: The First Giant Step
The Apollo 5 Mission
Bridge to Space (Apollo 6)
The Flight of Apollo 7
Apollo 8: Go for TLI
Apollo 9: Three to Make Ready
Apollo 10: To Sort Out the Unknowns
The Flight of Apollo 11: Eagle Has Landed
Apollo 12: Pinpoint for Science
Apollo 13: Houston, We've Got a Problem
Apollo 14: Mission to Fra Mauro
Apollo 15: In the Mountains of the Moon
Apollo 16: Nothing So Hidden
Apollo 17: On the Shoulders of Giants (a.k.a. *The Last Moon Landing*)

Places to Visit

Most aviation and space museums have Apollo exhibits. Here is a list of museums where the larger artifacts—the command modules, Saturn V rockets, moon suits, and other items can be found.

National Air and Space Museum
Independence Avenue & Sixth Street, SW
Washington, DC 20560
https://airandspace.si.edu
Apollo 11 CM *Columbia*, Skylab 4 CM, lunar rover, F-1 Engine, Apollo 11 MQF, and many Apollo artifacts.

Kennedy Space Center

SR 405

Kennedy Space Center, FL 32899

www.kennedyspacecenter.com

Apollo 14 CM *Kitty Hawk*, Apollo 8 Firing Room, Saturn V rocket, Shepard's Apollo moon suit, Apollo LM, Lunar Theater, and Rocket Park.

Space Center Houston

1601 NASA Parkway

Houston, TX 77058

https://spacecenter.org

Aldrin's moon suit visor, Apollo 11 survival kit, Saturn V injector plate, Apollo 17 CM hatch, and Apollo moon glove.

US Space & Rocket Center

One Tranquility Base

Huntsville, AL 35805

www.rocketcenter.com

Apollo 16 CM *Casper*, Saturn V rocket, and Rocket Park.

California Science Center

700 Exposition Park Drive

Los Angeles, CA 90037

https://californiasciencecenter.org

Apollo-Soyuz CM, Gemini 11 capsule, Mattingly's Apollo 16 space suit, and the Space Shuttle *Endeavour*.

San Diego Air & Space Museum

2001 Pan American Plaza

San Diego, CA 92101

http://sandiegoairandspace.org

Apollo 9 CM *Gumdrop*, Gemini capsule mock-up, and Mercury capsule mock-up.

Cosmosphere

1100 N. Plum Street

Hutchinson, KS 67501

http://cosmo.org

Apollo 13 CM *Odyssey*, Apollo space suits, Apollo 11 moon rock, and Apollo White Room.

(left) **Space Center Houston.** *Courtesy of Library of Congress, LC-HS503-4126*

(right) **Mural at the National Air and Space Museum.** *Courtesy of Library of Congress, LC-HS503-4210*

Museum of Flight
9404 E. Marginal Way South
Seattle, WA 98108
www.museumofflight.org
Apollo 17 LM mock-up, Apollo CM test module, and lunar rover mock-up.

Armstrong Air & Space Museum
500 Apollo Drive
Wapakoneta, OH 45895
www.armstrongmuseum.org
Armstrong's backup Apollo space suit, Gemini 8 capsule, Gemini 8 space suit, and moon rock.

National Museum of the US Air Force
1100 Spaatz Street
Wright-Patterson AFB, OH 45443
www.nationalmuseum.af.mil
Apollo 15 CM *Endeavour*, Gemini capsule, and Mercury capsule.

Museum of Science & Industry Chicago
5700 S. Lake Shore Drive
Chicago, IL 60637
www.msichicago.org
Apollo 8 CM and Aurora 7 Mercury capsule.

Virginia Air & Space Center
600 Settlers Landing Road
Hampton, VA 23669
www.vasc.org
Apollo 12 CM *Yankee Clipper* and Apollo LM simulator.

Frontiers of Flight Museum
6911 Lemmon Avenue
Dallas, TX 75209
www.flightmuseum.com
Apollo 7 CM.

Cradle of Aviation Museum
Charles Lindbergh Drive
Garden City, NY 11530
www.cradleofaviation.org
Apollo LM.

USS *Hornet*
707 W. Hornet Avenue
Alameda CA 94501
www.uss-hornet.org
Apollo test capsule, Gemini test Capsule, and Apollo 14 MQF.

Author's collection

NOTES

NASA recorded every word said by astronauts and ground controllers during the Mercury, Gemini, and Apollo missions. Every quote in this book, if made during a flight, has been taken from the mission transcripts found at www.jsc.nasa.gov/history/mission_trans/mission_transcripts.htm. If the quote you're looking for does not appear below, refer to the mission transcripts.

Many quotes below come from the Johnson Space Center Oral History Project (JSCOHP), found at www.jsc.nasa.gov/history/oral_histories/participants.htm.

For the remaining quotes, it is not uncommon for unrecorded conversations to be remembered differently by those who were present. I have generally chosen the quote from the source closest to the subject being discussed.

Introduction: One Long Step

"Sometimes it seems that Apollo": Eugene Cernan and Don Davis, *Last Man on the Moon: One Man's Part in Mankind's Greatest Adventure* (New York: St. Martin's Griffin, 1999), 344.

1. The Challenge

"Now is the time": John F. Kennedy, "Special Address to Congress on Urgent National Needs, 25 May 1961," John F. Kennedy Presidential Library and Museum, accessed April 19, 2018, www.jfklibrary.org/Asset-Viewer/Archives/JFKPOF-034-030.aspx.

"I thought he [Kennedy] was crazy": *Apollo 8: Christmas at the Moon*, directed by Dr. Elliott Haimoff (2003; Beverly Hills, CA: Global Science Productions, 2008), DVD, at (00:02:07).

"My interest in space travel": David Meerman Scott and Richard Jurek, *Marketing the Moon: The Selling of the Apollo Lunar Program* (Cambridge, MA: MIT Press, 2014), 2.

"He directed my thoughts": John Noble Wilford, *We Reach the Moon: The* New York Times *Story of Man's Greatest Adventure* (New York: Bantam Books, 1969), 37.

"I imagined how wonderful": Chris Gainor, *To a Distant Day: The Rocket Pioneers* (Lincoln: University of Nebraska Press, 2008), 38.

"Well, comrades": Gainor, *To a Distant Day*, 152.

"The Congress hereby declares": National Aeronauts and Space Act of 1958, Pub. l. no. 85-568, 72 Stat. 426-2, www.gpo.gov/fdsys/pkg/STATUTE-72/pdf/STATUTE-72-Pg426-2.pdf.

"Intelligence without genius": Colin Burgess and Kate Doolan, *Fallen Astronauts: Heroes Who Died Reaching for the Moon*, rev. ed. (Lincoln: University of Nebraska Press, 2016), 143.

"*Don't be afraid!*": Jesse Skinner, "Life on Mars?" *Toro*, October 14, 2008.

"*We are behind*": Wilford, *We Reach the Moon*, 80.

"*Boy, what a ride!*": Burgess and Doolan, *Fallen Astronauts*, 144.

"*The only complaint*": Wilford, *We Reach the Moon*, 80.

"*I was just devastated*": Simon A. Vaughan, "Worth the Wait," in *Footprints in the Dust: The Epic Voyages of Apollo, 1969–1972*, ed. Colin Burgess, (Lincoln: University of Nebraska Press, 2010), 276.

"*The women did*": Heather S. Deiss, "Katherine Johnson: A Lifetime of STEM," NASA, November 6, 2015, www.nasa.gov/audience/foreducators/a-life time-of-stem.html.

"*Mother and Dad barnstormed*": JSCOHP Walter M. Schirra Jr., December 1, 1998, 3.

"*[It was] the most natural*": Burgess and Doolan, *Fallen Astronauts*, 162.

"*I had my first ride*": JSCOHP Thomas P. Stafford, April 23, 2015, 2.

"*I lived in the country*" . . . "*go there one day*": JSCOHP Russell L. Schweickart, October 19, 1999, 1.

"*It occurred to me*": David Sheridan, "How an Idea No One Wanted Grew Up to Be the LEM," *Life*, March 14, 1969, 22.

"*Your figures lie!*": Deborah Cadbury, *Space Race: The Epic Battle Between America and the Soviet Union for Dominion of Space* (New York: Harper Perennial, 2006), 261.

"*The exploration of space*": John F. Kennedy, "Rice University Address," in *Footprints in the Dust: The Epic Voyages of Apollo, 1969–1972*, ed. Colin Burgess, (Lincoln: University of Nebraska Press, 2010), xxx–xxxii.

"*Everybody was working*": JSCOHP Janet M. Evans, August 7, 2003, 3.

"*You could stand across*": JSCOHP Neil A. Armstrong, September 19, 2001, 80.

2. Project Gemini

"*Anything that creeps*": Michael Collins, *Flying to the Moon: An Astronaut's Journey*, rev. ed. (New York: Square Fish, 1994), 33.

"*When the order came*": Burgess and Doolan, *Fallen Astronauts*, 184.

"*We hit the water*": JSCOHP James A. McDivitt, June 29, 1999, 41.

"*floating garbage can*": Francis French and Colin Burgess, *In the Shadow of the Moon: A Challenging Journey to Tranquility, 1965–1969* (Lincoln: University of Nebraska Press, 2007), 48.

"*Isn't it gorgeous?*": Miguel Acoca, "Success—and Yet Another Conrad Splashdown," *Life*, September 10, 1965, 38.

"*When I saw him*": Acoca, "Success," 38.

"*It was a real high*": JSCOHP Frank Borman, April 13, 1999, 13.

"*It was a great disappointment*": JSCOHP Armstrong, 2001, 54.

"*They wanted him to go*": JSCOHP Thomas P. Stafford, October 15, 1997, 19.

"*His face was pink*": JSCOHP Stafford, 1997, 23.

"*John made it look easy*": French and Burgess, *In the Shadow of the Moon*, 107.

"*trying to tie your shoelace*": Richard F. Gordon Jr., foreword to *Footprints in the Dust: The Epic Voyages of Apollo, 1969–1972*, ed. Colin Burgess, (Lincoln: University of Nebraska Press, 2010), xviii.

"*By the time we came out*": Billy Watkins, *Apollo Moon Missions: The Unsung Heroes* (Westport, CT: Praeger, 2006), xxii.

3. Tragedy and Triumph

"*There's been a problem*": James R. Hansen, *First Man: The Life of Neil A. Armstrong* (New York: Simon & Schuster, 2005), 306.

"*I thought you might*": Lily Koppel, *The Astronaut Wives Club: A True Story* (New York: Grand Central Publishing, 2013), 164.

"*Martha, I'd like to talk*": Burgess and Doolan, *Fallen Astronauts*, 204.

"*Mike, I think I know*": Koppel, *Astronaut Wives Club*, 165.

"*There's been an accident*": Koppel, *Astronaut Wives Club*, 163.

"*And here it was, 1967*": JSCOHP R. Walter Cunningham, May 24, 1999, 24.

"*We knew that it was bad*": JSCOHP Cunningham, 1999, 24.

"*How are we going*": George Leopold, *Calculated Risk: The Supersonic Life and Times of Gus Grissom* (West Lafayette, IN: Purdue University Press, 2016), 246.

"*Fire!*": Leopold, *Calculated Risk*, 250.

"*We've got a fire*": Leopold, *Calculated Risk*, 250.

"*We have a bad fire*": Leopold, *Calculated Risk*, 250.

"*I've never seen a facility*": William E. Burroughs, *The Infinite Journey: Eyewitness Accounts of NASA and the Space Age* (New York: Discovery Books, 2000), 76.

"*I can't tell you*": Leopold, *Calculated Risk*, 255.

"*We've lost the crew*": Leopold, *Calculated Risk*, 261.

"*The death of these brave*": Burgess and Doolan, *Fallen Astronauts*, 206.

"*Could the lives*": Eugen Reichel, *Project Apollo: The Early Years, 1960–1967* (Atlgen, PA: Schiffer Publishing, 2016), 139.

"*I remember being*": *The Wonder of It All*, directed by Jeffrey Roth (2009; Hollywood, CA: Indican Pictures, 2012), Blu-ray, at (00:20:42).

"If we die": Burgess and Doolan, *Fallen Astronauts*, 118.

"The guys who are going": David Scott and Alexei Leonov, *Two Sides of the Moon: Our Story of the Cold War Space Race* (New York: Thomas Dunne Books, 2004), 208.

"We are confident": Frank Bormon with Robert J. Sterling, *Countdown: An Autobiography* (New York: Silver Arrow Books, 1988), 180.

"We were given the gift of time": JSCOHP Armstrong, 2001, 60.

"My God": Douglas Brinkley, *Cronkite* (New York: Harper, 2012), 339.

"This was a disaster": Jeffrey Kluger, *Apollo 8: The Thrilling Story of the First Mission to the Moon* (New York: Henry Holt and Company, 2017), 108.

"I want to let you guys know": Walter Cunningham, *The All-American Boys: An Insider's Look at the Space Program and the Myth of the Super Hero* (New York: Macmillan, 1977), 16.

"Apollo 7 became very important": JSCOHP Cunningham, 1999, 29.

"As the months went by": Guenter Wendt and Russell Still, *The Unbroken Chain* (Burlington, Ontario: Apogee Books, 2001), 109.

"Space: the final frontier": *Star Trek* original series opening credits, posted on YouTube by Smithsonian National Air and Space Museum, October 13, 2016, www.youtube.com/watch?v=4pptCGR9N4g.

"It's as blue": Cunningham, *All-American Boys*, 121.

"It was quite windy": Cunningham, *All-American Boys*, 119.

I'VE DEVELOPED A NEW PHILOSOPHY: Koppel, *Astronaut Wives Club*, 198.

"OK, Cunningham": Cunningham, *All-American Boys*, 125.

"You don't really know": Cunningham, *All-American Boys*, 126.

"Within a short time": Cunningham, *All-American Boys*, 127.

FROM THE LOVELY APOLLO ROOM: John Bisney and J. L. Pickering, *Moonshots and Snapshots of Project Apollo: A Rare Photographic History* (Albuquerque: University of New Mexico Press, 2015), 16.

KEEP THOSE CARDS AND LETTERS: Bisney and Pickering, *Moonshots and Snapshots of Project Apollo*, 16.

"The last several days": JSCOHP Cunningham, 1999, 36.

"I spent a good part": Donn Eisele, "It Was a Pretty Fast Six-Handed Game for a While," *Life*, December 6, 1968, 61.

"Walt Cunningham would make": Wally Schirra with Richard N. Billings, *Schirra's Space* (Annapolis, MD: Bluejacket Books, 1988), 204.

"I was bored to tears": JSCOHP Schirra, 42.

"How do you feel?": Cunningham, *All-American Boys*, 142.

"even our clothes seemed heavy": Cunningham, *All-American Boys*, 144.

"These guys'll never fly again": JSCOHP Cunningham, 1999, 41.

4. To the Moon and Back

Jeez, there's got to be: Burroughs, *Infinite Journey*, 81.

"invoke Christopher Columbus": Burroughs, *Infinite Journey*, 81.

"Are you out of your mind?!": Robert Kurson, *Rocket Men: The Daring Odyssey of Apollo 8 and the Astronauts Who Made Man's First Journey to the Moon* (New York: Random House, 2018), 45.

"If these three men": *Earthrise: The First Lunar Voyage*, directed by Kevin Michael Kertscher (2013; Big Ocean Entertainment/Indigo Studios/WTTW/American Experience/PBS, 2014), DVD, at (00:23:06).

"We want to change" . . . *"Yes"*: Bormon with Sterling, *Countdown*, 189.

"almost turned handsprings": Alan Shepard and Deke Slayton, *Moon Shot: The Inside Story of America's Race to the Moon* (Atlanta, GA: Turner Publishing, 1994), 229.

"I was elated!": JSCOHP James A. Lovell Jr., May 25, 1999, 27.

"the fact that we were": *Earthrise*, Kertsche, at (00:06:58).

"Isn't this what": Robert Zimmerman, *Genesis: The Story of Apollo 8* (New York: Dell, 1998), 217.

"I can't go" . . . *"Would you believe, the moon?"*: Kurson, *Rocket Men*, 43

"After a careful": Bormon with Sterling, *Countdown*, 190.

"As much as I tried": *Earthrise*, Kertsche, at (00:28:12).

"We'd say how proud": *Earthrise*, Kertsche, at (00:28:25).

"OK, how's fifty-fifty?": Koppel, *Astronaut Wives Club*, 208.

"I'm going to name": Zimmerman, *Genesis*, 4.

"We talked and talked": JSCOHP Borman, 1999, 30–31.

"People stop talking": Anne Morrow Lindbergh, "The Heron and the Astronaut," *Life*, February 28, 1969, 22.

"As we lifted off": Andrew Chaikin with Victoria Kohl, *Voices from the Moon: Apollo Astronauts Describe Their Lunar Experiences* (London: Viking Studio, 2009), 20.

"I don't want to see": Andrew Chaikin, *A Man on the Moon: The Voyages of the Apollo Astronauts* (New York: Penguin Books, 2007), 88.

"For us this [day]": Shepard and Slayton, *Moon Shot*, 230.

"You could've heard": Watkins, *Apollo Moon Missions*, 163.

"You had to pinch yourself": JSCOHP Lovell, 1999, 30.

"I think we all started": Watkins, *Apollo Moon Missions*, 163.

"I just can't get over it": Zimmerman, *Genesis*, 76.

"So? Are we Go": James Lovell and Jeffrey Kluger, *Apollo 13* (New York: Houghton Mifflin, 1994, 2000), 47.

"God, there were stars": Chaikin with Kohl, *Voices from the Moon*, 36.

"These things seemed": *Earthrise*, Kertsche, at (00:42:54).

"To me [it] looked": Burroughs, *Infinite Journey*, 80.

"We came all this way": Matthew D. Tribbe, *No Requiem for the Space Age: The Apollo Moon Landings and American Culture* (New York: Oxford University Press, 2014), 80.

"the most influential": Zimmerman, *Genesis*, 284.

"It made us realize": Robert Jacobs, Michael Cabbage, Constance Moore, and Bertram Ulrich, eds. *Apollo: Through the Eyes of the Astronauts* (New York: Abrams, 2009), 33.

"We were like three school kids": *Earthrise*, Kertsche, at (00:45:22).

"I've never seen this place": *Earthrise*, Kertsche, at (00:51:45).

To MARILYN. MERRY CHRISTMAS: Kluger, *Apollo 8*, 258.

"I kept thinking of Jules Verne": Jim Lovell, "Earth, We Are Forsaking You for the Moon," *Life*, January 17, 1969, 29.

"The orange color changed": Burroughs, *Infinite Journey*, 83.

"When the main chutes": Bormon with Sterling, *Countdown*, 218.

"Hey, Apollo 8" . . . "made of American cheese!": Chaikin, *Man on the Moon*, 133.

"the precision of your": Bormon with Sterling, *Countdown*, 219.

"Accept, Mr. President": Kluger, *Apollo 8*, 279.

"To the crew of Apollo 8": Bormon with Sterling, *Countdown*, 220.

"The first flight": JSCOHP Schweickart, 1999, 17.

"I looked at Rusty": JSCOHP McDivitt, 1999, 68.

"If you barf": JSCOHP Schweickart, 1999, 30.

Are we going to have . . . "of the decade": JSCOHP Schweickart, 1999, 30–31.

"I don't know if": Wilford, *We Reach the Moon*, 208.

My job right now: JSCOHP Schweickart, 1999, 33.

Who am I?: JSCOHP Schweickart, 1999, 34.

"[Because of] the space program": JSCOHP Schweickart, 1999, 35.

"We figured we're not going": JSCOHP Schweickart, 1999, 37.

"I figured part of my job": JSCOHP Schweickart, 1999, 39.

"There are too many": Shepard and Slayton, *Moon Shot*, 242.

No way: Chaikin, *Man on the Moon*, 153.

"Only now did we finally get": Tom Stafford with Michael Cassutt, *We Have Capture: Tom Stafford and the Space Race* (Washington, DC: Smithsonian Books, 2002), 125.

"Well, now that we're here": Tom Stafford, "Apollo 10's Happy Trip to the Moon," *Life*, June 20, 1969, 42.

"We became like three": Cernan and Davis, *Last Man on the Moon*, 210.

"Don't get lonesome": Jay Barbree, "Live from Cape Canaveral": Covering the Space Race, from Sputnik to Today* (New York: Smithsonian Books, 2007). 151.

"You'll never know": Cernan and Davis, *Last Man on the Moon*, 214.

"After days in zero G": Cernan and Davis, *Last Man on the Moon*, 222.

"Eight years ago yesterday": Wilford, *We Reach the Moon*, 237.

51 DAYS TO LAUNCH: Cernan and Davis, *Last Man on the Moon*, 228.

5. The *Eagle* Has Landed

"We were at Cocoa Beach": Burroughs, *Infinite Journey*, 86.

"As far as I could see": Colonel Edwin E. "Buzz" Aldrin Jr. with Wayne Warga, *Return to Earth* (New York: Random House, 1973), 218–219.

"You're it, guys": Aldrin with Warga, *Return to Earth*, 201.

"Buzz went to work": Aldrin with Warga, *Return to Earth*, 201.

"I wish Buzz were a carpenter": Gene Farmer, "Buzz Aldrin Has the 'Best Scientific Mind We Have Sent into Space,'" *Life*, July 4, 1969, 24.

"You will not believe" . . . "to the rest of us": JSCOHP Dee O'Hara, April 23, 2002, 21–22.

GOOD BETWEEN ANY: Wendt and Still, *Unbroken Chain*, 132.

"Liftoff! We have a liftoff": Watkins, *Apollo Moon Missions*, 119.

"This is the last day": Andrew Smith, *Moondust: In Search of the Men Who Fell to Earth* (New York: Harper Perennial, 2005), 33.

"Today is our day": Gene Kranz, *Failure Is Not an Option: Mission Control from Mercury to Apollo 13 and Beyond* (New York: Simon & Schuster, 2000), 283–284; NOTE: There are many different reported versions of this speech, as no recording exists; this version is from Kranz's memoirs.

"We're Go on that alarm": Kranz, *Failure Is Not an Option*, 288.

"You'd better remind them": Shepard and Slayton, *Moon Shot*, 25.

"Charlie, shut up": JSCOHP Charles M. Duke Jr., March 12, 1999, 22.

"I was so happy": Domenica Di Piazza, *Space Engineer and Scientist Margaret Hamilton* (Minneapolis, MN: Lerner Publications, 2018), 6.

"*The Apollo flight software*": NASA Press Release 03-281, September 3, 2003, www.nasa.gov/home/hqnews/2003/sep/HQ_03281_Hamilton_Honor .html.

"*I kept shaking my head*": Koppel, *Astronaut Wives Club*, 226.

"*You could have rolled*": Mike Pohlen, interviewed by author, May 16, 2017.

"*That moment really united*": Scott and Leonov, *Two Sides of the Moon*, 248.

"*It was very cramped*": Aldrin with Warga, *Return to Earth*, 233.

"*I'll probably just say*": Watkins, *Apollo Moon Missions*, 21.

"*No, it made me feel*": Smith, *Moondust*, 57.

"*I thought a lot*": Michael Collins, "I Rattled Around in My Mini-Cathedral," *Life*, August 22, 1969, 29.

"*I realized that*": Jacobs, Cabbage, Moore, and Ulrich, eds., *Apollo*, 65.

"*I handled them*": Collins, "I Rattled Around," 27.

"*I carried prayers*": Collins, *Carrying the Fire*, 331.

"*This is the greatest week*": Wilford, *We Reach the Moon*, xvii.

"*Welcome home!*": Collins, *Carrying the Fire*, 447.

"*Daddy, it's summer vacation*": Aldrin with Warga, *Return to Earth*, 15.

"*We landed*": Burroughs, *Infinite Journey*, 91.

"*The tinsel is tarnished*": Aldrin with Warga, *Return to Earth*, 38.

"*Pete and I could*": JSCOHP Richard F. Gordon Jr., June 16, 1999, 55.

"*Flight, try S-C-E*": Watkins, *Apollo Moon Missions*, 164.

"*We were afraid*": JSCOHP Gerald D. Griffin, March 12, 1999, 11.

"*There wasn't a lot*": Nancy Conrad, *Rocketman: Astronaut Pete Conrad's Incredible Ride to the Moon and Beyond* (New York: New American Library, 2005), 170.

"*Let's go over it again*": Conrad, *Rocketman*, 172.

"*See ya tomorrow*": Conrad, *Rocketman*, 172.

Will I ever see this guy: Chaikin with Kohl, *Voices from the Moon*, 50.

"*Wow, this is scary*": Smith, *Moondust*, 196.

"*I couldn't see*": Pete Conrad, "We Just Went from Storm to Storm," *Life*, December 19, 1969, 33.

"*Everything was going great*": Alan Bean, "Pete Set It Down with a Firm Crunch," *Life*, December 19, 1969, 36.

"*Like most 'space food'*": Alan Bean, *My Life as an Astronaut* (New York: Minstrel, 1988), 74.

"*I had a job*": JSCOHP Gordon, 1999, 59.

"*You don't have to worry*": JSCOHP Gordon, 1999, 66.

"*Well, I don't know*": Smith, *Moondust*, 89.

"*Would you like to fly*" . . . "*what we're doing*": Chaikin with Kohl, *Voices from the Moon*, 116.

"*Dick, what the hell?*" . . . "*ship like that, Pete*": Conrad, *Rocketman*, 183.

"*As the heat builds*": JSCOHP Richard F. Gordon Jr., October 17, 1997, 30.

Wasn't it wonderful: Smith, *Moondust*, 347.

6. "Houston, We've Had a Problem"

"*thick soupy vapor*": Kranz, *Failure Is Not an Option*, 310.

"*We've got more than a problem*": Lovell and Kluger, *Apollo 13*, 95.

"*the command module's*": Kranz, *Failure Is Not an Option*, 314.

"*When that accident*": JSCOHP Griffin, 1999, 28.

"*[It] became very clear*": JSCOHP Fred W. Haise Jr., March 23, 1999, 32.

"*When you leave this room*": Kranz, *Failure Is Not an Option*, 321.

"*Within minutes, people started*": Chaikin with Kohl, *Voices from the Moon*, 142.

"*What do you mean?*" . . . "*astronaut I know*": Koppel, *Astronaut Wives Club*, 244.

"*OK, Joe, give them a call*": Burroughs, *Infinite Journey*, 97.

"*I have never experienced*": Chaikin, *Man on the Moon*, 335.

"*Our mission was a failure*": Shepard and Slayton, *Moon Shot*, 273.

"*I won't be making*": Shepard and Slayton, *Moon Shot*, 281.

"*Watch your ass*": Shepard and Slayton, *Moon Shot*, 278.

"*I could hear the rocket*": Edgar Mitchell, *Earthrise: My Adventures as an Apollo 14 Astronaut* (Chicago: Chicago Review Press, 2014), 75.

"*It felt like being*": Mitchell, *Earthrise*, 3.

"*Just between you and me*" . . . "*You'll never know*": Shepard and Slayton, *Moon Shot*, 305.

"*With a checklist*": Mitchell, *Earthrise*, 111.

"*Did you hear that?*" . . . "*I sure did*": Mitchell, *Earthrise*, 116.

"*you immediately start feeling better*": Chaikin with Kohl, *Voices from the Moon*, 111.

"*If we had thrown a rock*": Douglas MacKinnon and Joseph Baldanza, *Footprints: The Twelve Men Who Walked on the Moon Reflect on Their Flights, Their Lives, and the Future* (Washington, DC: Acropolis Books, Inc., 1989), 87.

What a beauty: Mitchell, *Earthrise*, 128.

"*Who's there?*": Mitchell, *Earthrise*, 134.

"*I had a ringside seat*": Mitchell, *Earthrise*, 138.

7. The Science Missions

"We'd spent years learning": JSCOHP Thomas K. Mattingly II, November 6, 2001, 65.

"He was thrilled" . . . *That's the spirit of Apollo*: JSCOHP Mattingly, 2001, 65–66.

"When [the technicians] closed": James B. Irwin and William A. Emerson Jr., *To Rule the Night: The Discovery Voyage of Astronaut Jim Irwin* (Philadelphia: A. J. Holman Company, 1973), 29.

"he had watched it": Scott and Jurek, *Marketing the Moon*, 120.

"like a piano tied": Cernan and Davis, *Last Man on the Moon*, 270.

"Hello, Earth—": Alfred M. Worden, *Hello Earth: Greetings from* Endeavor (Los Angeles, CA: Nash Publishing, 1974), 48–49.

"I just figured it": Chaikin with Kohl, *Voices from the Moon*, 174.

"When we opened the hatch": Irwin and Emerson, *To Rule the Night*, 99.

"I get into the raft": Irwin and Emerson, *To Rule the Night*, 110.

"was as keyed up": Charlie and Dotty Duke, *Moon Walker: The True Story of an Astronaut Who Found That the Moon Wasn't High Enough to Satisfy His Desire for Success* (Nashville, TN: Oliver Nelson, 1990), 18.

"We love you" . . . *"close to you"*: Duke, *Moon Walker*, 55.

"Our hearts sank": JSCOHP Duke, 1999, 19.

"When we leveled off": JSCOHP Duke, 1999, 33.

"You are floating": Duke, *Moon Walker*, 81.

"It was an incredibly beautiful": Duke, *Moon Walker*, 80.

"spaghetti bowl full of cables": JSCOHP Duke, 1999, 50.

"Going up Stone Mountain": JSCOHP Duke, 1999, 46.

"It was awesome": Chris Wright, *No More Worlds to Conquer: Sixteen People Who Defined Their Time—And What They Did Next* (London: The Friday Project, 2013), 51.

"We kept jogging": JSCOHP Duke, 1999, 51.

"This is the family": JSCOHP Duke, 1999, 64.

"I was in trouble": JSCOHP Duke, 1999, 54.

"If my spacesuit splits": Wright, *No More Worlds to Conquer*, 50.

"The more you waited": Bisney and Pickering, *Moonshots and Snapshots of Project Apollo*, 164.

"Ken, I've got": Duke, *Moon Walker*, 218.

"Apollo 17 may be the last": Chaikin, *Man on the Moon*, 505.

"It's lighting up the sky!": Chaikin, *Man on the Moon*, 500.

"[The] valley where we were to land": JSCOHP Eugene A. Cernan, December 11, 2007, 3.

"Long before that": JSCOHP Cernan, 2007, 4.

"Who wants to go": Chaikin with Kohl, *Voices from the Moon*, 102.

"You look back at": Burroughs, *Infinite Journey*, 103.

"I was having a ball": Chaikin with Kohl, *Voices from the Moon*, 122.

"There's a fundamental": *Man on the Moon*, with Walter Cronkite, CBS News (1981; New York: Timeless Media Group, 2014), at (01:13:30).

"Both sides of the street": JSCOHP Evans, 2003, 20.

Epilogue: The End of Apollo

"I do know deep down": Robert Pearlman, "Epilogue: Souvenirs of Small Steps," in *Footprints in the Dust: The Epic Voyages of Apollo, 1969–1972*, ed. Colin Burgess, (Lincoln: University of Nebraska Press, 2010), 425.

"Looking back at that": Irwin and Emerson, *To Rule the Night*, 17.

"When I looked back": Ron Judd, "With a View from Beyond the Moon, an Astronaut Talks Religion, Politics, and Possibilities," *Seattle Times*, December 7, 2012, www.seattletimes.com/pacific-nw-magazine/with-a-view-from-beyond-the-moon-an-astronaut-talks-religion-politics-and-possibilities/.

"I now felt a strong": Mitchell, *Earthrise*, 152.

"If you can't be good": Tara Dixon-Engel and Mike Jackson, *Neil Armstrong: One Giant Leap for Mankind* (New York: Sterling, 2008), 24.

INDEX